Assessing and Promoting Writing Skills

New Edition

Jean Alston

NASEN

A NASEN PUBLICATION

First published in 1993

Revised edition published in 1995

ISBN 0 906730 71 6

NASEN

Published by NASEN Enterprises Ltd.
NASEN Enterprises Ltd. is a company limited by guarantee, registered in England and Wales. Company No. 2637438

Further copies of this book and details of NASEN's other publications may be obtained from the Publications Department at its registered office:
2, Lichfield Road, Stafford, ST17 4JX. (Tel: 01785 46872; Fax: 01785 41187)

Cover design by Graphic Images. Tel: (01782) 49301

Typeset in Palatino and printed in Great Britain by Impress Printers (Stoke-on-Trent) Ltd.

Assessing and Promoting Writing Skills

CONTENTS

Acknowledgements

The author and publishers wish to express their gratitude to:

- statisticians at The Cheshire County Research and Intelligence Unit for assembling statistical information from which a cohort of schools was established;

- pupils and teachers from 17 Cheshire primary schools who provided samples of writing during the 1980s;

- John Machin, headteacher; classteachers Wendy Davies, Isabel Clutton and Pansy Smith, and pupils at Wood Lane County Primary School, North Staffordshire, all of whom participated in an extensive writing project during the Summer Term, 1992. Also to John Machin and Isabel Clutton who allowed the author to conduct group teaching in 1994;

- Mike Hinson and members of the NASEN Publications Sub-Committee for their editorial help and advice;

- Prue Wallis Myers for her artwork;

- Melvyn Ramsden for permission to reproduce two figures from his publication, *Rescuing Spelling;*

- William Murray for his permission to use the Key Words to Literacy on page 49 from the publications: *Key Words to Literacy and the Teaching of Reading* by J. McNally and W. Murray, The Teacher Publishing Co, Kettering (revised 1968), and *Key Words to Reading,* M. Murray and J. Corby, Ladybird Books, Loughborough, 1991;

- Cedric Croft of the New Zealand Council for Educational Research for permission to include the list of *Commonly Misspelt Words;*

- Felicitie Barnes and Beverly Scheib for advice on microtechnology.

CHAPTER 1

Introduction

This book is about the children who make a start in their earlier school years but rarely go on to enjoy writing or to have pride in what they achieve. It is much less about able children's writing, as much has been written in that vein. It shows that with intelligent observation, information about different aspects of writing, and a sympathetic approach, teacher and pupils can work together to raise the standards and aspirations of less able and those regarded as more or less average writers in school. Teachers who adopt the ideas presented here will be able to ensure that pupil writers 'move on' with their writing, and that those who remain at an inordinately low level of performance are fewer than we have expected in recent and earlier times.

Writing standards

Reading standards, teaching and assessment have received considerable attention in recent years and continue to do so in the mid 1990s. Writing, in contrast, is rarely given the attention it deserves. Research shows that a sizable proportion of pupils of all ages have problems with writing. The evidence is as follows:

- In the 1988 Assessment of Performance Unit Survey of more than 2,000 pupils at 11 and 15 years of age, of those at primary level, 20 per cent of boys and 10 per cent of girls claimed that they 'hated writing'; 37 per cent of boys and 23 per cent of girls claimed that they wrote as little as possible, and only wrote when they had to (APU, 1991).

- In a study of teaching strategies and pupil performance at Key Stage One, the authors stated as follows:

> 'While attention was being focused on the diagnosis and 'remedial' teaching of reading, the pressing need for similar work with reference to the teaching of writing has not been widely recognised. 'A 'WRITING RESCUE' programme would apply to a larger proportion of pupils than those who have difficulty learning to read'.
>
> (Cato et. al. NFER, 1992)

Many children have low standards in reading and writing throughout their school lives and often become disaffected in consequence. For these children, help with writing will encourage reading and writing to improve together, so that standards in both can be raised. Some low attainers read to age appropriate levels but seem unable to catch up in writing and spelling. For these pupils, improved writing will help to bridge the attainment gap. Pupils are often judged by how or what they write, and are assessed for National Curriculum and examination purposes by the quality of their writing. It is imperative, therefore, that they should be helped to achieve their potential.

Writing is a very complex skill and teachers often do not know how to assess it. In the national survey, *Assessment, Recording and Reporting; a Report by HMI on the First Year* (1991), HMI concluded that four out of five teachers were failing to appreciate that pupils' written work can be just as valuable as specially prepared tests when it comes to assessment. They reported as follows:

> 'Pupils' written work in the core subjects is potentially a large source of evidence of achievement . . . in over 80 per cent of schools inspected marking provided only an overall impression of the quality of the work and, too often, pupils' work went unmarked'.

So pupils write for much of the school day and teachers learn very little from their writing.

'Putting pen to paper' is clearly a problem for many pupils, and the ability or opportunity to assist them is not always within the province or reach of teachers. Pupils who are competent writers will have access to the many-faceted school curriculum and will achieve their full potential. The good readers who write inadequately and those who do not succeed in the wider range of literacy skills will cope badly in the educational system and in employment in later years. Participation in social, cultural and artistic circles is greatly curtailed if one cannot participate at a literate level of communication. Above all, writing is closely associated with self concept - it is a little of ourselves on paper which others can take away with them. Improving writing may well enhance a feeling of well-being and, ultimately, improve behaviour.

At a conservative estimate, pupils write for thirty or so per cent of the school day, depending upon their age. In total, this amounts to thousands of hours in a normal school life span. In spite of this large investment in writing time, a sizable proportion of pupils leave school with minimal writing skills, and will have experienced little enjoyment from their writing tasks. In this book, the author hopes to show how pupils can be taught competent handwriting, spelling and grammatical skills, and how they can progress to instructive, experimental, and creative writing. Competent and interesting writing can be a joy to pupils and teachers alike and enhances all aspects of communication, educational or otherwise.

Improving writing skills

The sequence followed in this text is hierarchical, i.e. it recognises that writers need at all times to be craftsmen. They need to know that letters are formed in specific ways and that letter joins cannot be made unless the directions in which letters are written are accurate. They need to know that each word has a correct spelling or letter sequence, even though they will not be expected to be entirely accurate during their early years in school. Later they will learn that writing needs a structure of sentences, paragraphs, and other presentation formalities. As writing skills develop, other aspects of punctuation will help to make writing more expressive and sophisticated.

Chapter 2, a new section for this revised edition, outlines six guiding principles for developing writing skills in reluctant writers. It outlines the special needs of pupils with potential writing problems, the strategies which they can be taught to improve writing skills to enhance self-concept, also teaching principles which can be adopted by teachers in order that intervention will be most effective.

The general foundation of correct formation, a degree of spelling competence, a growing word bank for writing, and an ability to write in sentences together make up the secretarial skills which are essential for the development of logical, stylistic and expressive writing.

Alongside the development of secretarial skills, grammatical, logical, stylistic and expressive aspects of writing will be generated. Gradually the writer will recognise and utilise the formalities of written language which complement, though may differ from, those of spoken language. Chapters 12 and 13 deal specifically with grammatical, logical, stylistic and expressive features. The general view expounded here is that if the craft or skills of writing are neglected in the early stages, it is often our least able pupils who suffer most and who may never go on to be competent writers. When writing development is based on firm foundations, pupils across the complete ability range are likely to benefit. However, the teacher is urged to be flexible, to always begin with encouraging words, and to introduce changes little by little, in a constructive manner.

Chapter 8 suggests an assessment/teaching model for the busy class teacher. A Teacher's Assessment Sheet and two pupils' assessment sheets are photocopiable examples for the teacher to use when assessing his or her own pupils' writing. Chapter 16 draws attention to the importance of word processing as an enabling and/or enhancing medium, particularly, though certainly not exclusively, for those less adept with paper and pencil. An appraisal of books and resources completes the text.

All sections of the text are in accordance with, rather than following precisely, the School Curriculum and Assessment Authority's proposals for National Curriculum English programmes of study. The new and concise National Curriculum Orders will be implemented as from September, 1995 and will be in force until the year 2,000 (and perhaps beyond). Teachers are required to teach according to National Curriculum requirements but, within these strictures, are encouraged to consider the progress that pupils make, and to reassess their approaches as they see the need to do so. The Orders indicate that pupils' writing is expected to improve but do not always indicate the precise teaching approaches through which changes can be brought about. This book includes suggestions for teaching strategies which can be used to supplement Programmes of Study guidelines. Only the Programmes of Study are referred to, rather than former, more contentious level descriptions.

CHAPTER 2

Developing Writing Skills

It seems that many pupils learn to write relatively well and without undue difficulty. These tend to be the children who: learn to speak when we expect them to; listen to stories; have normal concentration levels, and who develop pencil and paper skills that are within normal limits.

Less able writers may have few of these normal patterns of development and may also have limited reading competence. There are also pupils who read relatively well but who fail miserably in writing and spelling.

Both groups of pupils will benefit from the structured approaches suggested here. However, for those with specific writing and spelling difficulties, the introduction of a structured and sequential language programme and the adoption of truly multisensory strategies are likely to lead to the greatest benefit and progress.

Six principles are suggested as being the most important for the development of writing skills. They include reference to pupils' special writing needs, to particular aspects of the writing curriculum, to strategies that pupils can be taught to improve writing skills, and to principles that can be adopted by teachers so that intervention can be most effective.

1 - The major requirement is complete mastery of the 26 letters of the alphabet, paying particular attention to vowels.

Appendix B (on page 118 - 123) is a photocopiable resource from which letter cards can be made. These cards can be used for teaching by the teacher, and can be handled and retained by the pupil during the learning period. The greatest benefit is obtained by showing the letter symbol side first, and turning the card quickly so that the picture clue gives reward, whether the child has named the letter or not. Letter sounds are learned first until the child can say 'c...cat', and so forth in response to the symbol stimulus only. The stimulus cards are presented as letters ready for joining, i.e. in accordance with the early joining required for progress at National Curriculum Key Stage One.

Letter names can also be taught in readiness for spelling progress.

The small marks indicate where letters should begin for correct letter formation in handwriting.

Details of further use for these cards are given in the chapters referring to the teaching of spelling and handwriting.

2 - Pupils are able to make little progress unless they have a written word bank from which words for writing can be readily recalled.

The first groups of Key Words (see page 49) should form a good part of this word bank, and clearly words such as 'the', 'and', 'is', 'was' 'in' are useful words to know. Nevertheless, all pupils will develop their own words for writing, however limited. Their attention should be drawn to their own word bank, and they should be taught how to add other words as their general literacy skills improve.

Sarah has a very limited personal word bank, as can be seen from the example of her free writing in *Figure 1*. Nevertheless, it is important that she knows of this nucleus and is encouraged to record them in her own way, e.g. in a personal word box, book, or small chart that can be placed on her desk. To produce the word bank, elicit a piece of free writing, e.g. 'My Favourite Person'. Trace over the correctly spelt words and extract them to show the personal word bank, as shown in *Figure 2*. The word bank words and new ones that are added can be used to teach joined writing, and for the practise of spelling strategies that will eventually be utilised in the learning of new words.

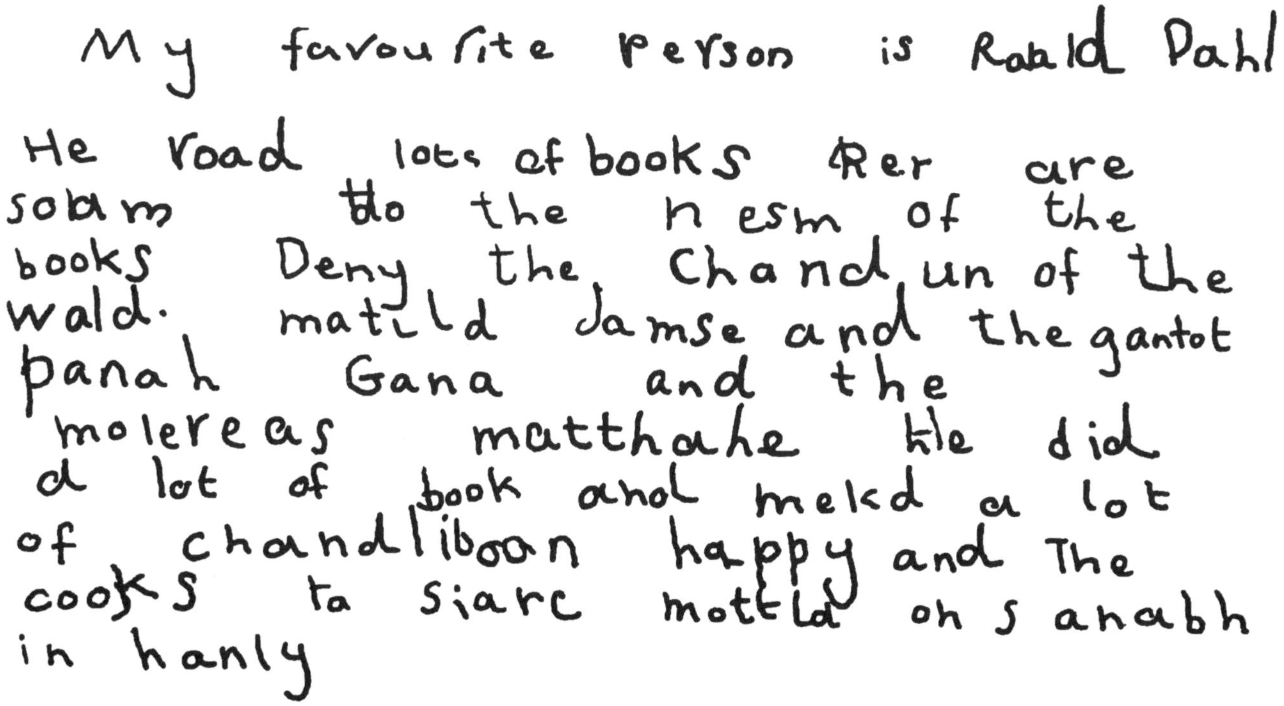

Figure 1 - Sarah' writing about her favourite person.

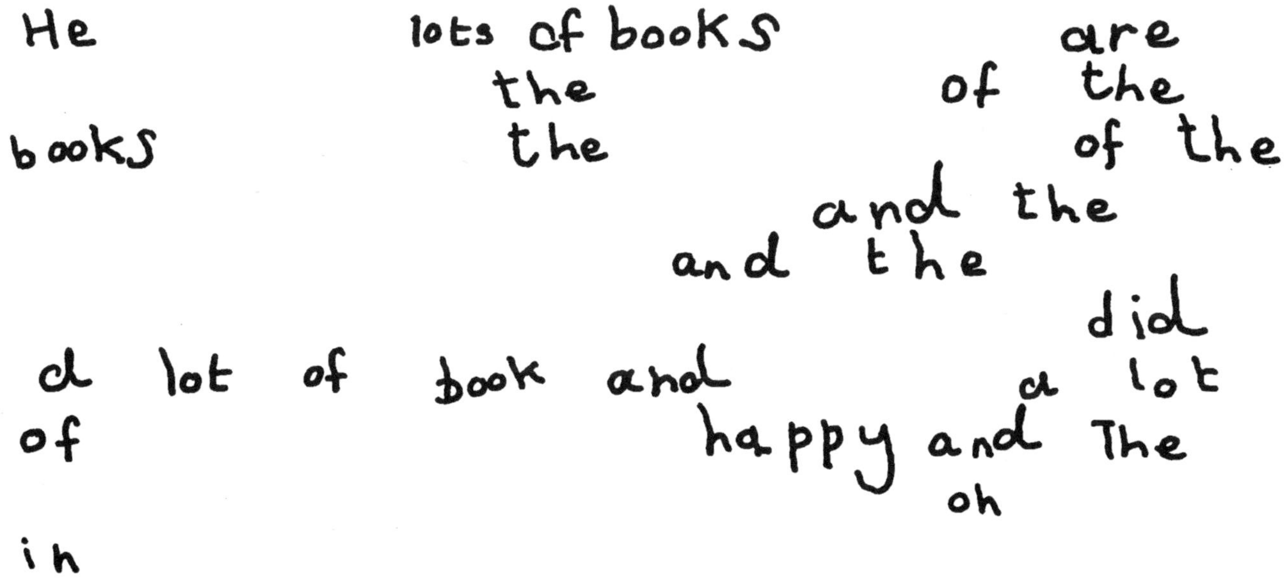

Sarah's personal word bank;

He	lots	of	books	are	the	and
lot	book	did	happy	in	on	a

Figure 2 - Sarah's correctly written words, i.e. the nucleus of her personal word bank.

3 - Less able writers needs 'props', particularly in the early stages.

'Props' are constructs that will help writers. They are ones which they will learn to recognise as a source for their own writing. The letter cards referred to in Principle 1 are props, words on cards from their own bank are props, and so are:

- charts which have limited information such as days of the week, or words related to 'the house', 'the farm', or 'the seaside';

- a Key Word card, or a 200 word dictionary;

- worksheets on which the required words or sentences are printed at the foot of the page, as in Oxford Workbooks, or in some worksheets and workbooks available from Learning Materials Ltd.

However, there is a great danger that pupils might depend too heavily on worksheets and workbooks which have all the words available for them. At each stage, they should always be encouraged to write a number of the words with eyes closed, or to retain them by looking at the word, saying the word, and writing it from memory.

4 - The integration of speaking, reading, and writing is essential to progress.

The pattern of learning is that young children learn to speak by listening to the language around them. They go on to develop speech and language by participation and by being read to. They begin, even if poorly on occasion, to read themselves. Up to this stage, overt speech is always involved. Writing, however, is somehow expected to be different, and children write in silence. As they progress, they are instructed to read through their own writing, but rarely are they told to 'read aloud'. Reading one's own writing aloud is the key to writing and spelling progress; it allows writing to become fully integrated with the language, listening, speech and reading that have gone before. As is stated in the National Curriculum English order, 'Intonation leads to punctuation'. However, the full benefit cannot be reaped unless the intonation is clearly heard aloud, and becomes the pupil's own transfer from the speaking to the writing process. Pupils must be encouraged to **read their writing aloud**, even if a special class time has to be put aside, when all the pupils can do so.

5 - Stronger senses and skills should aid weaker ones to facilitate learning.

The value of a multisensory teaching approach was established, certainly as early as 1943, when Grace Fernald wrote her seminal text, *Remedial Techniques in Basic School Subjects.* The term 'multisensory' refers to the involvement of all senses in the learning process, the view being that if one of more of the senses are weak, the stronger senses can be employed to enhance learning. In practice, this means that looking, saying, listening, and writing are all overtly employed whenever new learning is required. Reading aloud ones own writing certainly has a multisensory element, and so do the strategies for learning new words which are outlined in the spelling chapter of this book.

Whenever the pupil has learnt a new word, new phrase, or new short sentence, saying it and writing it with eyes closed will ensure that learning becomes well established, and is likely to be retained for later retrieval from working memory.

6 - Focusing on one aspect of written output, helps pupils to understand what is required.

Much of this book is about intervention in pupils' writing, so that progress will occur. Writing is a very complex process. I suggest that the lack of progress in so many pupils' writing is due to its extreme complexity. Imagine the confusion that might occur in our less able writers when the teacher refers in turn to so many aspects. On one occasion, he or she might say, 'Your handwriting is untidy', later, 'Your spellings need greater attention' and then, 'You seem to be forgetting full stops, and capital letters for the new sentences'. These comments refer, of course, only to the simple aspects of writing - even then they are too much for those who find writing difficult. My way of dealing with this complexity is to point out to pupils that they should concentrate on one aspect, perhaps for a week, a fortnight or more, that is until progress has been made in that particular aspect of writing. This policy will allow the *teacher* to concentrate as well as the children. It will allow him or her to know where he or she should intervene and to clarify his or her thoughts in consequence. Of course, the other aspects of writing will still receive attention and may even make incidental progress. For the children, however, the lightening of the great load of working with written language may reap considerable benefits.

CHAPTER 3

Writing Progress in the Junior Years (Year 3 to Year 6)

It is now common practice for schools to keep samples of pupils' written work. The samples are likely to consist of whatever writing might be taking place at the time and might be 'best' written work, 'usual' written work, or a redraft of writing that is completed for a particular purpose. Standardised assessment is common for reading and spelling, and most teachers could quickly inform parents about progress that children have made in either of those subjects. Writing is usually a different matter, and even retained samples may be completed under different conditions so that comparison for assessing progress is particularly difficult. One way of overcoming the problem is to give the same task at different stages of the child's school life, as we do with normative reading and spelling tests.

An example of standardised assessment in writing is shown in Simon's work (*Figure* 3). He was given a standard task in the January of each of his junior school years (Year 3 to Year 6). The task was that he should write to the title 'My Favourite Person (or Personality)', that he should complete the task on paper measuring 205 millimetres long and 180 millimetres wide, that line ruling should be at 8 millimetre intervals, and that he should write for exactly 20 minutes. The dated samples were retained, so that when each year's writing was completed, the writing samples from the former year or years could be used for comparison.

Simon's writing was collected from a primary school by the current writer for research purposes, therefore school staff were unable to make comparisons as each sample was completed. Simon did not benefit from this research exercise but, with hindsight, the writing samples which follow indicate that he might have done so, had the samples been utilised in the ways described in the remainder of this book.

What happened to Simon's writing during his junior school years?
From a quick perusal, it is apparent that Simon's written work did not progress as much as might be desired in three years of junior school teaching. Recognition of his needs and intervention by the teacher could have led to much greater progress than the sequence of writing shows. The following comments indicate a few of Simon's strengths, some of his major weaknesses as demonstrated in the Year 3 sample, together with some ideas for teaching that might have led to progress. Teaching objectives are listed in possible order of priority.

Simon's writing in Year 3
Simon writes enthusiastically about his Liverpool football idol - we would not wish to curb this enthusiasm. He has the beginning of a reliable written word bank for spelling (even if he was helped with 'favourite' and 'person',) and he is able to spell words such as 'plays', 'and', 'good', 'some', and 'boots'. For a later teaching occasion, however, we should note that he does not:

- form letters correctly, particularly p, r, n, b, and d;

- know that 'x' height letters, and letters with ascenders should be at two different but consistent heights if the reader of his writing is to be able to read what the writer intends;

- write in sentences.

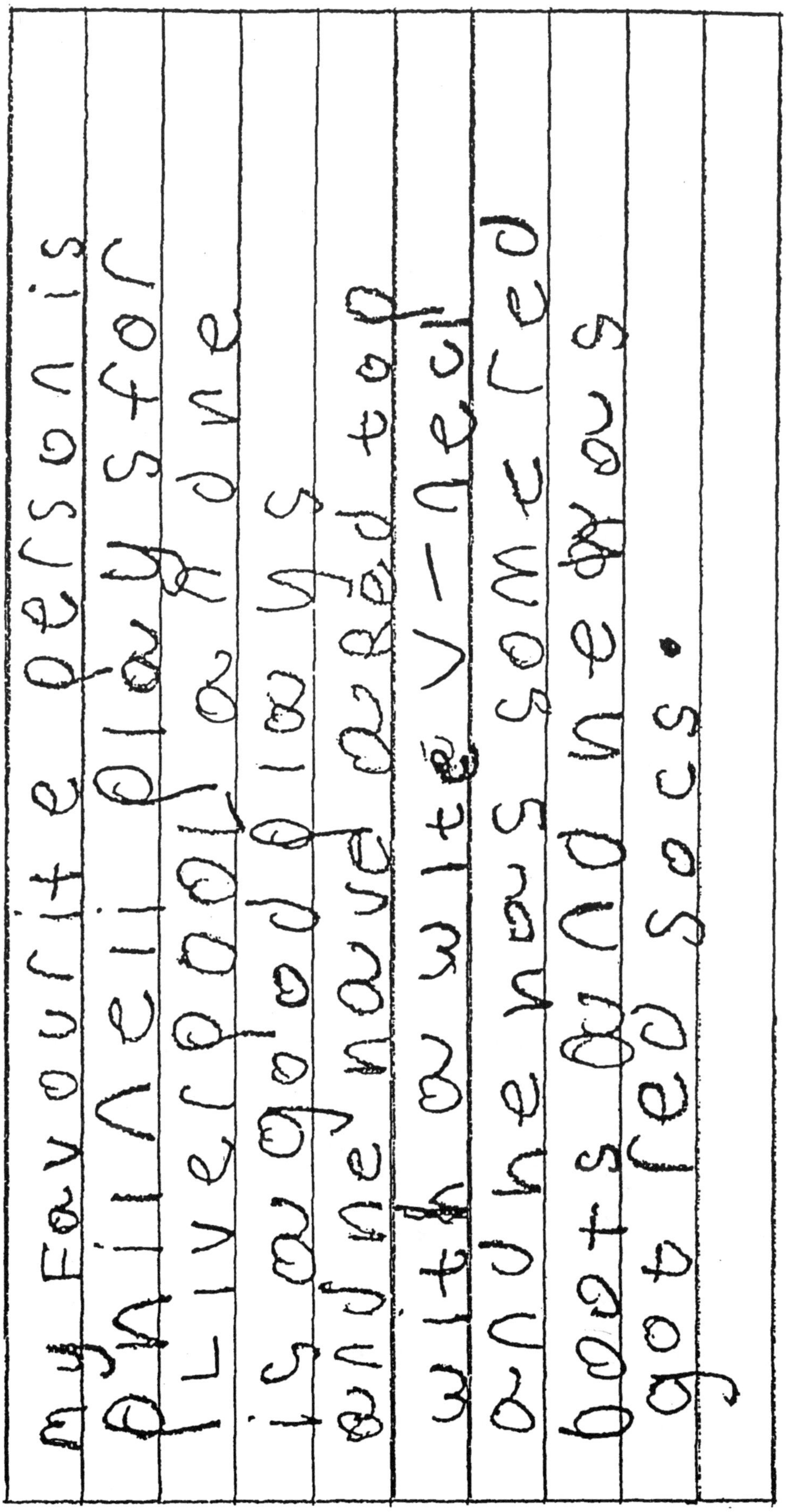

Figure 3 - Simon's writing in Year 3.

Teaching objectives in order of priority might be:

1. The proper formation of p, r, n, b and d - 'd begins like c' is a statement that he might remember easily. The letters p, r, n and b should all start at the top of the letter.

2. Differentiation between heights of: a c e i m n o r s u v w x z
   b d f h k l t
   g j p q y

Pencilling in an extra line at 'x' height will help him to differentiate letter heights.

3. Learning that each statement can be written as a sentence.
   A strip of paper for writing each statement will help him to see how each can be written on a strip, beginning with capital letter and ending with full stop.
   Written sentences will then be:

   My Favourite person is Phil Neil.
   He plays for Liverpool and he is a good player.
   He has a red top with a white V neck.
   He has some red boots and he has got red socks.

4. Encouraging him to recognise that he is able to spell a number of words correctly and that these will always be available to him when he is writing. As other commonly required words are learned they can be added to his own correct spelling word bank.

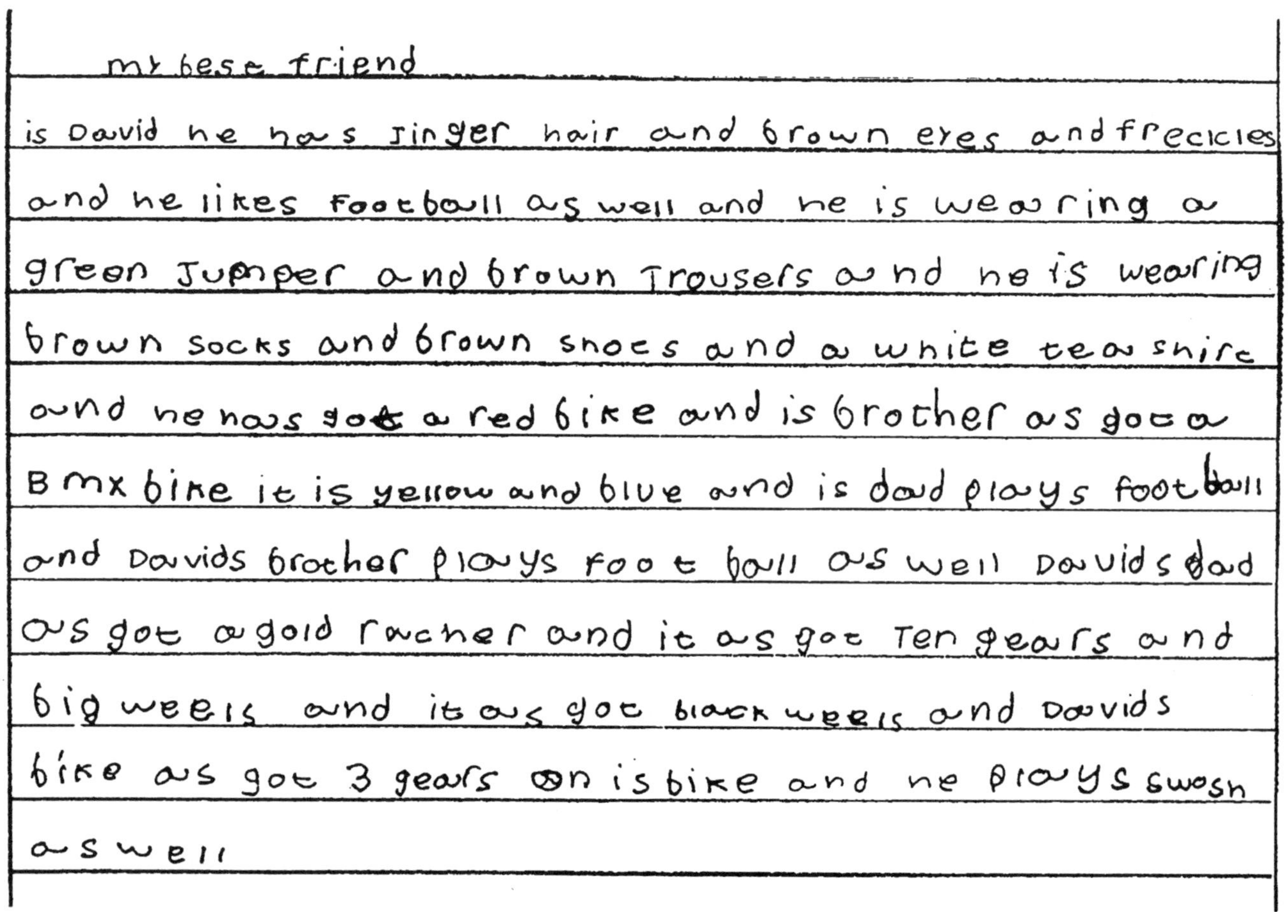
my bese friend
is David he has Jinger hair and brown eyes and freckles
and he likes Football as well and he is wearing a
green Jumper and brown Trousers and he is wearing
brown socks and brown shoes and a white tea shirt
and he has got a red bike and is brother as got a
Bmx bike it is yellow and blue and is dad plays football
and Davids brother plays foot ball as well Davids dad
as got a gold racher and it as got Ten gears and
big weels and it as got black weels and Davids
bike as got 3 gears on is bike and he plays swosh
as well

Figure 4 - Simon's writing in Year 4.

Simon's Year 4 writing indicates that he is making considerable progress in spelling. For example, his bank of correctly spelled words includes:

'likes' 'freckles' 'trousers' 'wearing' 'brother'.

Many of the handwriting difficulties evident at Year 3 are retained at Year 4. He still writes in continuous prose, with no indication of 'taking a breath' or punctuation.

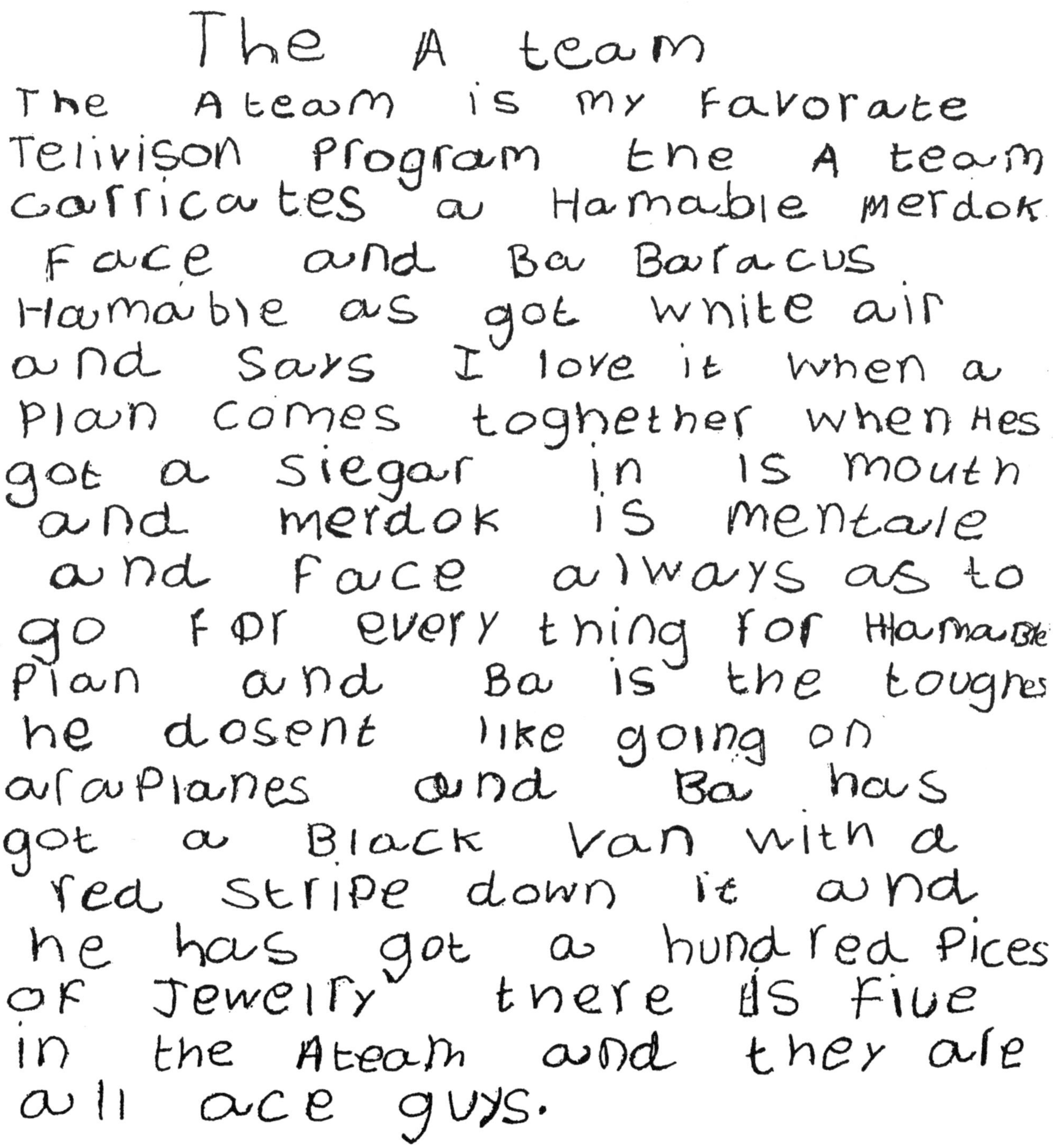

The A team

The A team is my favorate
Telivison program the A team
carricates a Hamable merdok
Face and Ba Baracus
Hamable as got white air
and Says I love it when a
plan comes toghether when Hes
got a siegar in is mouth
and merdok is mentale
and Face always as to
go For every thing for Hamable
plan and Ba is the toughes
he dosent like going on
araplanes and Ba has
got a Black van with a
red stripe down it and
he has got a hundred Pices
oF Jewelry there is five
in the Ateam and they ale
all ace guys.

Figure 5 - Simon's writing in Year 5.

Simon A-TeAm.

B.A. Barfacas

BA is tough when He Plays in the A-Team
and the words that uses are funny is
and. Hair is Black and is frelndly. I
like it when Hannibal Puts sleeping
Powder in is Drink of milk Because
he doset like Airaplanes or Boats
he likes drinking milk whall not
Always there are four in the A-TeAM
Tempolton Peck mad Murdock and
tough BA. and master of Descises is Hannib
BA. wears allot of Jewlery and is a
master of MAchanics Peck is the
who Always gos after girls and
always gets all the stuff for
the A-TeAm the series is good
I like it my dad likes and
my sister likes it to it is on
at 6oclock on saturday some
times I mis it or sometimes my
dad tapes it if we go out my
sister thinks B.A. is funny
to and I Do so Does my dad
But my mum likes corenation
street But I Dont like or my dad

Figure 6 - Simon's writing in Year 6.

Years 5 and 6 samples show that the spelling strengths apparent at Year 4 have not been built upon, so that the words 'telivison', 'carricates' and 'toghether' are incorrect in Year 5, and 'freindly', 'airaplanes', 'whell' and 'machanics' are incorrect in Year 6.

The continuous, unpunctuated prose employed in Year 3 continues in examples from the next three years. The continuous use of 'and' for joining statements diminishes in the Year 6 sample, when new statements may begin with 'I', the name of another character, 'sometimes' or 'but'.

Some of Simon's teaching requirements will also be suitable for other members of his year group. Some teaching objectives can be used for class lessons and others for a group of children. If learning does not occur, it does seem that, as in Simon's case, the major weaknesses of the Year 3 writers may be still apparent when pupils reach Year 6.

Figure 6 shows Simon's writing when he is nearing transfer to secondary education. A quick look at the four year sequence shows that letter formation had greatly improved in Year 5. However, attempts at joined writing in Year 6 were extremely flawed, and a reliable cursive writing programme was needed if Simon was to be adequately prepared for secondary education. Letter heights were still not always differentiated. Simon was beginning to try to join his letters but did not know how to do so. He had some unnecessary letter movements, evident in the words 'likes', 'drinking' and 'wears', and these, along with other handwriting difficulties, seemed to be affecting spelling and general writing skills.

Ensuing chapters of this book show how teaching intervention can improve the writing skills of pupils like Simon, as they progress through school. As previously stated, because written work is complex, it is suggested that there is concentration upon separate writing skills on different occasions, i.e. there is a time for focusing on handwriting, one for spelling, one for logical and stylistic writing, and so forth. By giving a week, fortnight, or month to each aspect of writing, the focus can be maintained and the general writing complexity will not detract from the focused teaching objectives established by teacher and pupil.

CHAPTER 4

National Curriculum Writing: Aspects of Assessment

Requirements of the National Curriculum and its assessment have dominated teachers' discussions for several years. However, after extensive consultation between the School Curriculum and Assessment Authority (SCAA) and teachers in 1994, the National Curriculum Orders, including Programmes of Study and attainment level descriptions, have been finalised for at least five years, i.e. until the year 2000 or beyond.

A general outline of National Curriculum Writing is presented here. More detailed aspects are presented in the five chapters of this book which refer to handwriting, spelling, punctuation, grammar, and logical, stylistic and expressive features of writing.

General principles

The Programmes of Study are intended to guide the planning, teaching and day-to-day assessment of pupils' work. The Order begins with an overview, or summary, of the General Requirements for the teaching and assessment of English. Later in the publication, requirements are presented within Key Stages, so that they can be read with pupil age range and achievement in mind. The overview is presented here to set the scene for the remainder of this text.

In each Key Stage and for each Programme of Study, there are three sections:

- Range;
- Key Skills;
- Standard English and Language Study.

A General Requirement is that pupils should be given opportunities to develop their understanding and use of standard English and to recognise that:

- standard English is distinguished from other forms of English by its vocabulary, and by rules and conventions of grammar, spelling and punctuation;
- the grammatical features that distinguish standard English include the way in which pronouns, adverbs and adjectives should be used and how negatives, questions and verb tenses should be formed. These features tend to be present in both spoken and written forms;
- compared with spoken language, writing is more permanent, often carefully crafted, and less dependent on immediate responses.

To develop as effective writers

Pupils should be taught to use:

- **compositional skills** - developing ideas and communicating meaning to a reader, using a wide-ranging vocabulary and an effective style, organising and structuring sentences grammatically and whole texts coherently;

- **presentational skills** - accurate punctuation, correct spelling and legible handwriting;

- a widening **variety of forms** for different purposes.

Key Stage One Programme of Study states that the range of pupils' experience of writing should include:

- an understanding of the value of writing as a means of remembering, communicating, organising and developing ideas and information, and as a source of enjoyment. They should be taught to write independently on subjects that are of interest and importance to them;

- opportunities to write in response to a variety of stimuli, including stories, poems, classroom activities and personal experience. They should be taught to identify the purpose for which they write and to write for a range of readers, e.g. their teacher, their family, their peers, themselves;

- presenting their writing in different ways, helpful to the purpose, task and reader. The range should include a variety of ***narratives,*** e.g. stories, diaries, poems; ***notes,*** e.g. lists, captions; ***records,*** e.g. observations; and ***messages,*** e.g. notices, invitations, instructions.

The Key Skills receive their appropriate attention within the separate chapters 9, 10, 11, 12 and 13 of this book.

Standard English and Language Study

Pupils should be introduced to the vocabulary, grammar and structures of written standard English. They should be taught to apply their existing linguistic knowledge, drawn from oral language and their experience of reading, to develop their understanding of the sentence and how word choice and order are crucial to clarity of meaning.

Key Stage Two Programme of Study states that the range of pupils' experience of writing should be extended to include:

- writing for varied purposes, understanding that writing is essential to thinking and learning, and that it is enjoyable in itself. They should be taught to use writing as a means of developing, organising and communicating ideas;

- opportunities to write for a widening range of readers, to include other children, adults in the school or community, and imagined audiences;

- characteristics of different kinds of writing, e.g. argument, commentary, narrative, dialogue. The forms in which they write should include imaginative writing, e.g. stories, poems, dialogues, drama scripts, diaries. Non-fictional writing should include reports, instructions, explanations, notes and letters.

Pupils should be taught to use features of layout and presentation.

Key Skills

Pupils should be given opportunities to plan, draft and improve their work on paper and on screen, and to discuss and evaluate their own and others' writing. To develop their writing, pupils should be taught to:

> ***plan*** - note and develop initial ideas;
>
> ***draft*** - develop ideas from the plan into structured written text;
>
> ***revise*** - alter and improve the draft;
>
> ***proof-read*** - check the draft for spelling and punctuation errors, omissions or repetitions;
>
> ***present*** - prepare a neat, correct and clear final copy.

Discussion

The compiler of National Curriculum, the School Curriculum and Assessment Authority, is concerned with the wide range of pupil achievement. Readers of this book who are principally concerned with pupils who have special educational needs will realise that, although the general requirements of National Curriculum English must be borne in mind, day-to-day programmes for their pupils will need to have much more limited aims and objectives than National Curriculum documents suggest. Throughout this text, I shall attempt to give ideas about how pupils with special needs can be assessed in a positive manner and how, with limited objectives and a delineation of skills so that both pupils and teachers are not overwhelmed by requirements, hesitant and less able writers can achieve much more than has been hitherto expected.

CHAPTER 5

A School Writing Policy

The essentials of a school writing policy will include the recognition that there are skills which are vital if pupils are to develop into competent writers. Handwriting, for example, requires the teaching of accurate letter movements if it is to become a useful tool for writing. If correct movements are not developed in the early stages, some children will be handicapped for the remainder of their school lives. Accurate movements from the beginning can prevent 11 years or more of corrective teaching.

Spelling

Spelling requires that letters have a specific sequence. Although English spelling may often seem unpredictable, if methods of learning to spell are taught, rather than pupils being presented with spelling lists without instruction about how to learn them, then the majority will be given the opportunity to spell with reasonable competence. Spelling methods should embrace the view that children have different strengths and weaknesses, and those with specific spelling difficulties may have difficulty remembering which letters follow which. Therefore, more than one way of learning to spell should be acknowledged in school.

Punctuation

The formalities of simple punctuation need to be taught. For example, sentences need to be meaningful statements which can be written separately but, eventually, can be joined to make meaningful paragraphs and sequential written texts. Intonation when speaking is our first guide to punctuation, and should be utilised to full advantage. Punctuation should first be discussed as it appears in reading books as this can be the source for guidance in reading expression. For example, a comma usually means a pause, fleeting or otherwise. A question mark or an exclamation mark is intended to influence reading intonation in a particular way. Attention can be drawn to all these features from time to time. Discussing the punctuation on the page of a simple reading book could form a useful subject for class or group discussion. Discussion with individual pupils about punctuation in their own reading books, i.e. at their own level of reading development, is a useful way of ensuring differentiated teaching.

Grammar

Grammatical skills tend to develop even more from the spoken word than the simpler writing skills already considered. Many less able pupils write as they speak for a longer period than their peers. Some adults with specific spelling and writing difficulties seem to show this characteristic throughout their adult lives. Comparison of spoken and written sentences is therefore an ongoing need for these writers. They can be asked to write a sentence as they say it and then to revise it so that it will make sense to a reader. Quite often there will be superfluous words such as 'got' and 'the' that can be omitted, colloquialisms that can be corrected, and occasional additions that are necessary because the reader may not always be in the speaker's presence.

A vocabulary of terms for discussing grammatical features seems to be needed if teacher and pupils are to have a common language for discussion. Nouns/names and proper nouns/proper names give guidance on the use of the initial capital letter. Knowledge of 'doing words'/verbs allow for discussion on past, present and future for those who have difficulty writing consistently within the same verb form. The terms 'conjunction' or 'joining word' allow for discussion about writing in sentences, joining together two of more short sentences, or about extending sentences so that more expressive or complex writing can ensure. More able writers can go on to learn about pronouns and adverbs. However, as with all teaching, the observant teacher will know when each child is ready to absorb each new piece of grammatical information.

A vocabulary for writing

Beyond the consideration of secretarial and simple discursive writing skills, the realm of general authorship now has a quite extensive vocabulary in schools. For example:

brainstorming
planning
drafting
composing
revising
reporting
reviewing
editing
collaborating
conferencing

Children's writing might indicate a repertoire of skills. For example, they might:

report
respond
reconstruct
narrate
argue
explain
recollect
hypothesise

Audience

An extremely important feature of current writing in schools is that there should be evidence of an audience. Of course, on many occasions the audience will be the teacher and classmates, but there will also be occasions when pupils can direct their writing to the rest of the school, to parents, neighbours, and the community at large. For example, is there a school newsletter? Can each class in turn be responsible for writing it? Who writes the letters to parents? Must it always be written by the headteacher or member of staff and typed by the school secretary? Do pupils in neighbouring schools write to each other, exchanging information about their gardens, outings, collection of information about weather and other activities? There may be a community project, demolition, new road, or other subject of common interest that could stimulate writing. This could be done in the form of a class booklet/news sheet, if individual communication seems to be less desirable. Headteachers and their members of staff are likely to meet and communicate from time-to-time, so why not the pupils? Local cafes, libraries, council offices and similar public buildings are sometimes willing to display writing from schools, and this gives an extra impetus to encouraging children to write rather better than usual.

However, even with all the possible outlets and audiences discussed above, much of writing is inevitably for oneself, so why not make it a record of each individual pupil's writing and show that it can be collected together and valued as an indication of progress in its own right?

School policy

A major requirement of a school policy is that it should arise out of discussion between all school staff and certainly should have their support. If there is a common vocabulary for discussing writing and an ongoing staff dialogue, then continuity of policy between classes, and the recognition of an associated hierarchy of writing skills is likely to occur. The recognition that children develop at different rates and need to be taught or reminded about different skills at different stages will make progress more likely, particularly for less able pupils. We are quite used to having individual pupils on different levels of reading (books, schemes, or worksheets), but we have made very little progress towards a differentiated approach to the teaching of writing. We assume that this is intrinsic in the very act of writing, i.e. as each child determines his or her own level of complexity and sophistication. However, as the writing samples in Chapter 3 indicate, this may mean that some pupils make little progress. Intervention and differentiation are clearly essential.

A writing policy: Agenda for discussion

1. How will pupils learn sounds, names and movements of the 26 letters of the alphabet?
2. Is there a common handwriting script throughout the school?
3. Will print be taught at all, at the early stages of writing, or will even the first letters have a small exit stroke ready for when joining can ensue?
4. Will there be a range of writing papers, with varying lined formats, so that the teacher can select as appropriate for each pupil's needs and progress?
5. Will there be a range of pencils, pens and pencil holders (e.g. stetro grips) for those who need them?
6. Can the links between reading and writing be fully utilised?
7. How will reluctant writers be encouraged?
8. Will pupils be introduced to spelling strategies, and what should those strategies consist of?
9. How can vocabulary and writing skills be extended?
10. Will writing be assessed and monitored in a standardised manner?
11. Can teaching differentiation be built into the programme wherever possible?
12. What will be the range of audience for pupils' writing?

Ensuing chapters show how basic skills and the more sophisticated writing strategies can, at different times, be identified, separated out and brought together again. In this way, pupils' writing and teachers' understanding can develop and flourish, operating sometimes at a simple level for precise teaching and sometimes at a sophisticated level to encourage the joy and satisfaction that competent writers experience.

CHAPTER 6

The Scope of Children's Writing

The subjects about which children write, and the modes or genres in which they write about them, are almost boundless. To suggest titles for such activities can be fraught with pitfalls. However, different types of writing give scope to the writer and assist the teacher to examine progress or otherwise in pupils' written work. The broad categories of chronological and non-chronological writing are not mutually exclusive as different writers may tackle subjects in different ways. However, they provide a starting point from which a more sophisticated examination of writing can ensue.

Chronological writing

Sequence of events

Write about a sequence of events, real or imagined, in other words a chronological account:

- 'My holiday'
- 'What I did on Saturday'
- 'My trip to the theatre'
- 'Our day at Alton Park'
- 'A day in the life of a dog'

Stories

Rewriting a known story. Creating stories, for example, adventures.
Writing stories for a known audience, for example, young children.

Letters

Informal letters to friends and relatives.
Formal letters to people not known in person.

Biography

My grandad/grandma.
My favourite person.
Someone I know very well.
My pet.

Autobiography

My life.
May I introduce myself?

Historical documents

These may have chronological elements, for example:
How people lived in Saxon times;
The lives of children in the year 1800.

Plans
Plans for, or reports of, scientific investigations, outings or events.

Poems may be chronological.

Extending chronological writing
Pupils can be helped to extend chronological writing so that it has:

- an opening;
- characters;
- a setting;
- a series of events;
- a leading towards a climax;
- a resolution or conclusion.

Enhancing chronological writing
Writing can be enhanced by:

- describing settings and contexts;
- describing the feelings of characters;
- describing actions;
- expressing attitudes and emotions;
- inventing fantasy through imaginative stories;
- trying to be amusing.

Non-chronological writing
Children's first writing can often be of a non-chronological kind, for example:

'My cat is black and white';

'I like my dog because he is friendly'.

However, this early non-chronological writing can become chronological as the writer becomes more proficient.

Examples of non-chronological writing

- invitations;
- lists;

- notices;
- notes for activities;
- posters;
- newspaper articles;
- reviews.

Some of the above may also have chronological sequence.

CHAPTER 7

Assessing Pupils' Writing

Two questions are addressed in this chapter:

- What will the children be writing about?

- What aspects of their writing should be assessed?

When their writing is to be assessed, pupils should be asked to write about a subject which they know well. This will preclude the situation where they spend more time thinking than writing.

As mentioned in an earlier chapter, the present author is greatly indebted to the staff and pupils of a Staffordshire primary school for their enthusiasm and whole-hearted involvement in a writing project. Standards of writing in this school proved to be high and its most able children wrote extensively with regard to both imaginative and informative writing. The information gathered from the project has provided examples which are relevant to the topic under consideration in this chapter.

Titles for children's writing

The class teachers and the author concluded that the following titles would give adequate choice. Some adaptations gave scope for the children to write about their own locality and experiences. (Readers of this book should not experience any difficulty in adapting these choices to their own situations.)

General titles

Titles that pupils might tackle because they require little other than everyday knowledge, include:

My favourite person

My favourite book

My favourite television programme

My favourite animal

My pet

I'd like to be ...

My favourite lesson

My village

England: describe England to someone who has never been here.

Hanley: describe Hanley to someone who has never been there.

Wood Lane: describe Wood Lane to someone who has never been there.

Wood Lane School: describe Wood Lane School to someone who has never been there.

Chronological and sequential writing

Titles to encourage chronological/sequential writing include:

My first day at school

My lucky day

The best day of my life

I'd like to be ...

A visit to the supermarket

A story for four-year-olds: once upon a time ...

A story for six-year-olds: once upon a time ...

One hundred years ago. You wake up in 1892 and describe a day in your life.

Imagine someone has never seen a swimming pool or the sea. Describe the water and how they could learn to swim.

A boy or a girl leaves home and catches a train to London. Describe what they do, what happens, and what they feel like.

Newspaper reports

A newspaper report will often be chronological. Pupils can be asked to write imaginary reports of the following:

The motorway crash

The collapse of a railway bridge

The runaway bull

The runaway horse

The thunderstorm

The rescue

The bank robbers

Letter writing

Letter writing is essential in many aspects of life. Adults often wish they could get their views noticed, and a good letter often achieves that purpose. Ask pupils to write to the newspaper about one of the following topics:

Improving the village

Making the village safer for young children

Making the village more interesting

Suggesting how the village can be protected from people who break into houses and/or cars

Imagine that a play area with swings, slides, roundabout and football field is going to be sold to someone who builds houses. Write to the newspaper or the council to protest.

Assessing aspects of writing

The second major question, 'What aspects of writing should be assessed?', relates to the parameters of writing. What aspects of writing are amenable to assessment, and how should we examine them?

At a more formal level, we have tended to consider that pupils should have legible handwriting, reasonably accurate spelling, good presentation and punctuation, adequate grammatical structure, and a logical stylistic and expressive written style. These requirements, once achieved, can help the writer to develop individuality in writing, and to engage the interest of anyone who reads his or her written work.

Writing is a very complex skill, as the suggested parameters show. It is more useful, in consequence, to assess each piece of written work in one aspect of performance, and to help the writer with one aspect at a time. Writing samples from two Cheshire junior school pupils are shown as examples. Perusal of each piece of writing will usually reveal the areas which need most attention, and lead to conclusions about the ways in which a writer can be helped to improve his or her skills. For example, the eight-year-old writer of *Figure 7*, needs help with aspects of handwriting legibility, such as spacing and letter size. The eleven-year-old writer of *Figure 8*, whilst remaining immature in handwriting, and in need of a cursive handwriting script, also needs help with presentation aspects such as paragraphing and logical writing skills. An introductory paragraph, such as the one which precedes the general description in *Figure 9*, makes the script far more meaningful to the reader, who may otherwise be uninformed about the content of the writing.

Figure 7

The immediate impression of the eight-year-old's writing is that the writer has much to write about his 'person'. He writes about his appearance, his family, and his birthday. The writer takes no 'breathing space' for punctuation, and does not organise the written content. Spelling is better than the general impression would indicate because he spells words like 'brother', 'jumper', 'likes', 'ginger' and 'cousin' correctly.

One is inclined to suggest that this writer is let down by his handwriting and that that should be the first aspect of writing development to be tackled. After that, the writer's correct spelling word bank could be assembled, and he could be shown how many words he has spelled correctly. The script could then be divided into sentences formed from the pupil's own script, either by writing statements on separate strips of paper, or by outlining each potential sentence by circling it with a pencil outline.

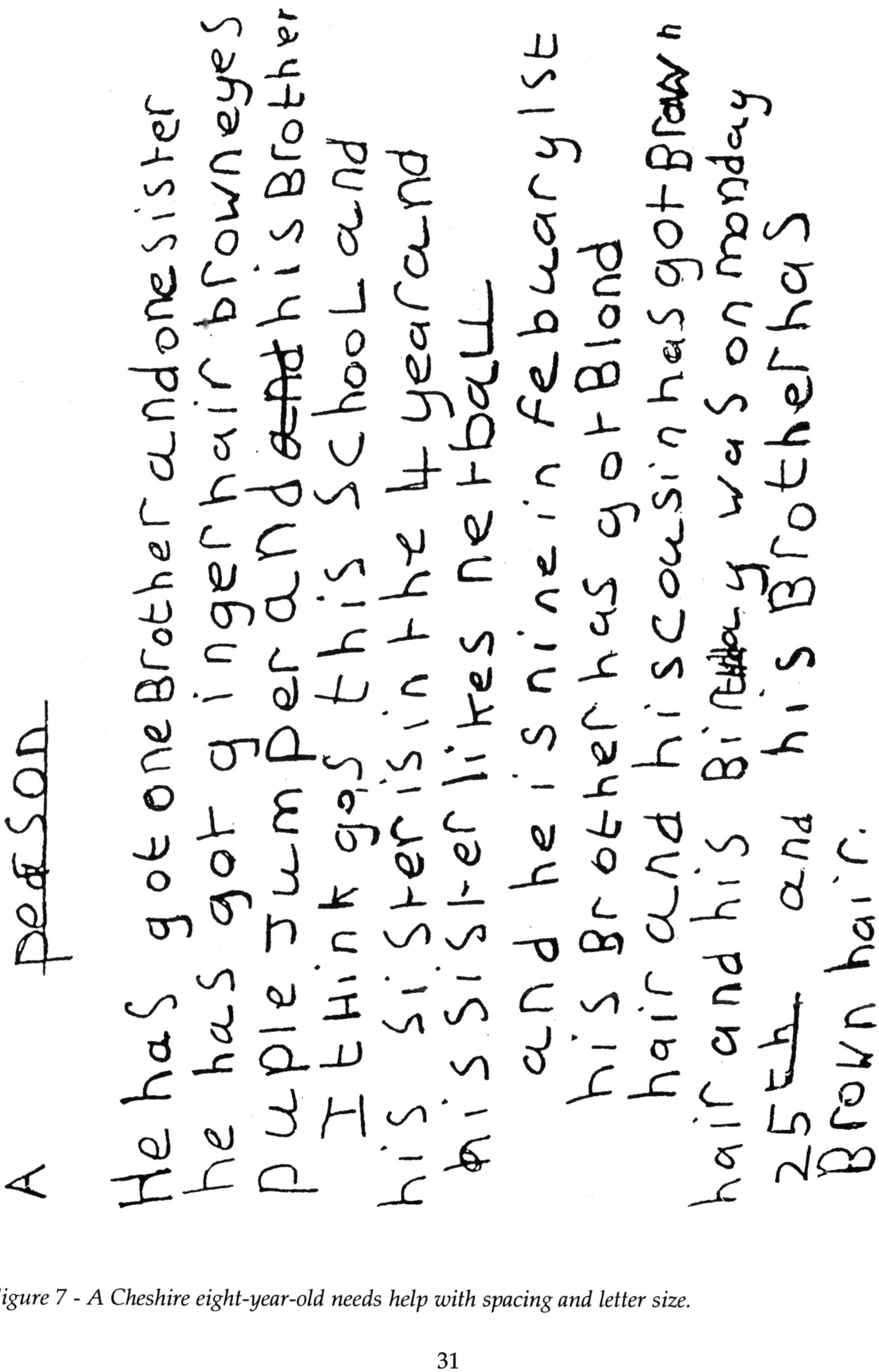

Figure 7 - A Cheshire eight-year-old needs help with spacing and letter size.

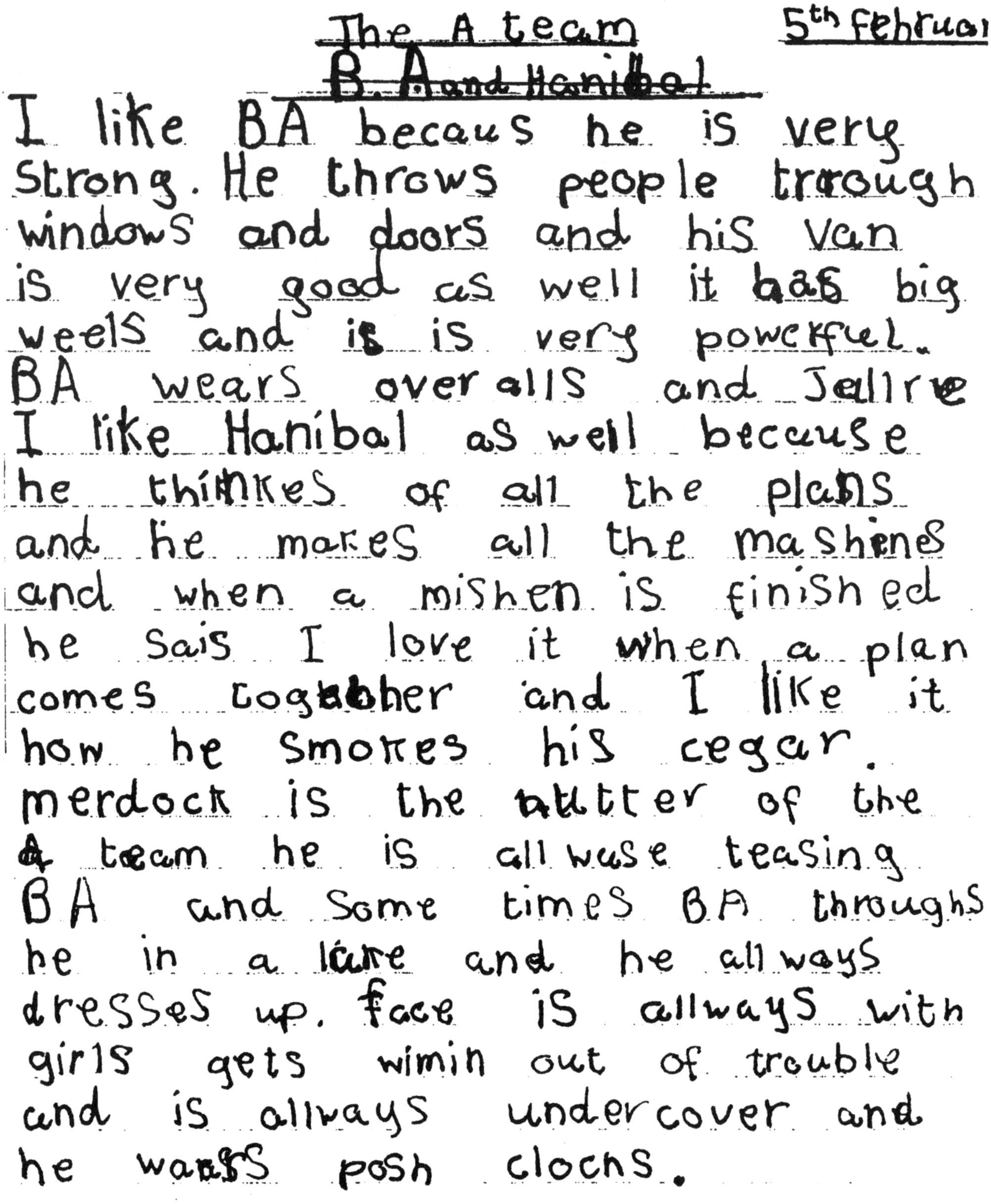
The A team 5th februar
~~B A and Hanibal~~
I like BA becaus he is very
Strong. He throws people trough
windows and doors and his van
is very good as well it has big
weels and is is very powerful.
BA wears over alls and Jallre
I like Hanibal as well because
he thinkes of all the plans
and he makes all the mashenes
and when a mishen is finished
he sais I love it when a plan
comes together and I like it
how he smokes his cegar.
merdock is the nutter of the
A team he is all wuse teasing
BA and Some times BA throughs
he in a lake and he allways
dresses up. face is allways with
girls gets wimin out of trouble
and is allways undercover and
he wears posh clocks.

Figure 8 - A Cheshire eleven-year-old needs help with paragraphs and writing sequence.

Figure 8

The eleven-year-old's writing shown in *Figure 8* indicates how unprepared he is for coping with the considerable writing demands of the secondary school curriculum. Reliance on print script for too many years has meant that he is likely to have great difficulty in developing a good adult cursive hand. He writes extensively about his favourite television personalities, but he is unable to organise the script into logical sequence and paragraphs.

Figure 9

Figure 9 is written by an adult who wished to illustrate how the writing in *Figure 8* could be improved. The cursive handwriting gives a more adult appearance, and the introductory paragraph prepares the reader for the information he will read in the rest of the script. Other than these revisions, the content is very much as the eleven-year-old wrote in the original script.

Conclusions

The general message from this short examination of two Cheshire pupils' writing is that for each pupil there may be one aspect of writing which needs attention first, or from which the pupil's written presentation will benefit most. When the major problem is corrected, some of the more minor aspects may seem to correct themselves. For example, an improvement in handwriting might allow a pupil to pay attention to sentence structure; the development of a cursive writing style might lead to a gradual improvement in spelling. Because writing is such a complex skill, difficulty with any aspect can place a heavy burden on the writer. The reduction in any aspect of this burden can free the writer to deal with other writing requirements.

The major lesson to be learnt from this exercise is that the teacher can develop an awareness of factors influencing general writing and its presentation. It is often relatively easy to see where the pupil's strengths and weaknesses lie, therefore, intervention with regard to a major problem can sometimes lead to spontaneous improvement in other writing skills.

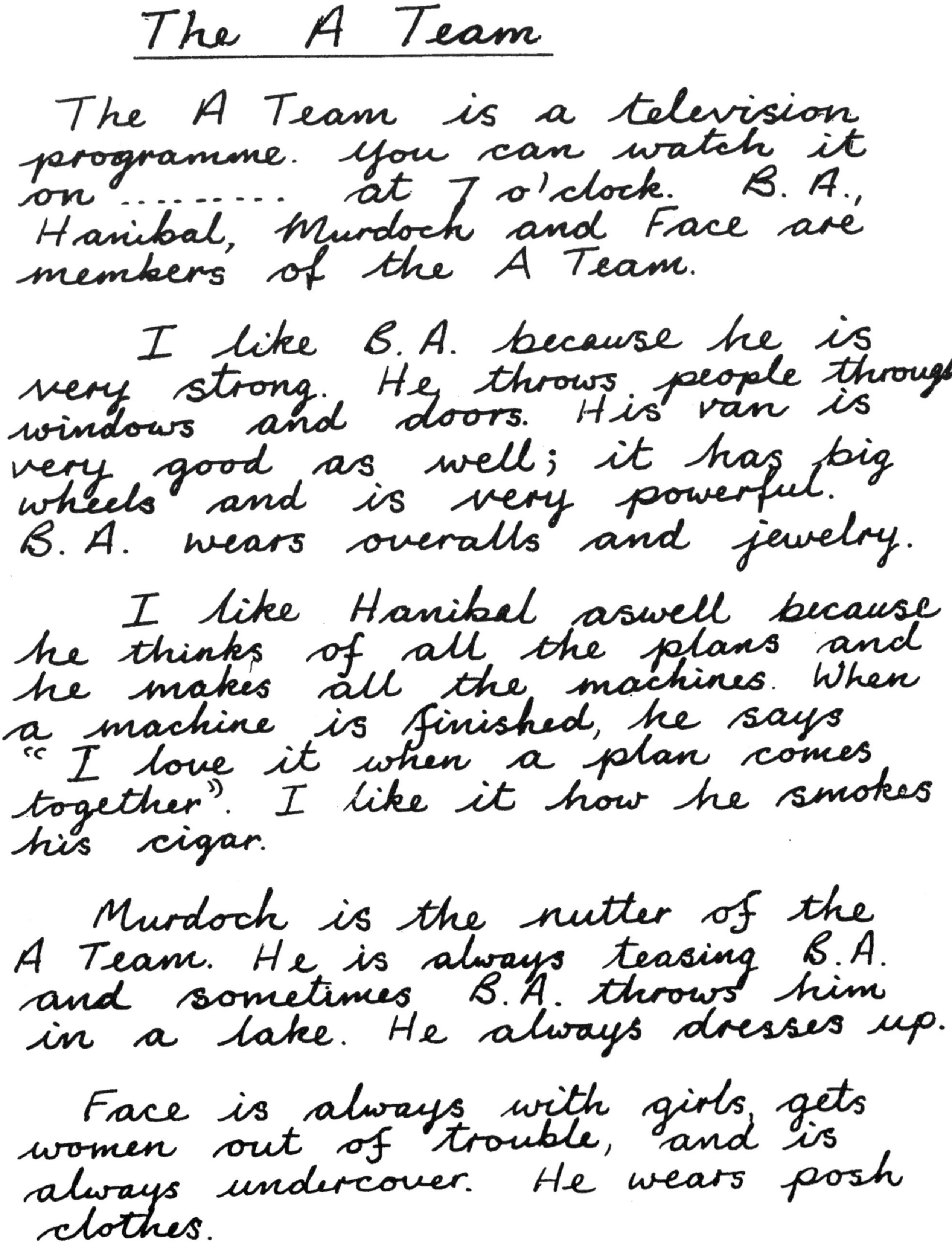

The A Team

The A Team is a television programme. You can watch it on .... at 7 o'clock. B. A., Hanibal, Murdoch and Face are members of the A Team.

I like B. A. because he is very strong. He throws people through windows and doors. His van is very good as well; it has big wheels and is very powerful. B. A. wears overalls and jewelry.

I like Hanibal aswell because he thinks of all the plans and he makes all the machines. When a machine is finished, he says "I love it when a plan comes together". I like it how he smokes his cigar.

Murdoch is the nutter of the A Team. He is always teasing B. A. and sometimes B. A. throws him in a lake. He always dresses up.

Face is always with girls, gets women out of trouble, and is always undercover. He wears posh clothes.

Figure 9 - This is what we would aim for in the eleven-year-old's writing.

CHAPTER 8

A Model for Assessment

Later in this book, Chapter 9 deals with handwriting, Chapter 10 deals with spelling, and Chapters 11, 12 and 13 with punctuation, grammar, and features of expression and style respectively. The selection of these five categories is hierarchical in the sense that the first identified skill is probably the least complex, providing a foundation for the skills which follow. Subsequent ones are each more demanding in their turn, with all skills being essential for the proper production of pupils' general written work. The choice of skills for assessment is also pragmatic, insofar as they appear to be the ones which emerge as a result of observing children's writing. They are categories which teachers use and which pupils can be taught to understand. It is not the author's purpose to lead the reader into the vernacular of linguistics or written language concepts, but to give practitioners a working model for assessing writing and for their subsequent intervention where individual difficulties become apparent.

The three major premises on which this book is based are:

1. Teachers' intervention as pupils progress through school can improve written work.

2. Because of the complexity of writing, assessment and intervention will best be implemented by dealing with each aspect separately and for a specific period of school time.

3. There need to be appropriate models for managing assessment and intervention strategies, such as those set out on pages 37, 38 and 39.

The **Teacher's Assessment Sheet** is suitable for teacher in-service education or school staff discussion and development. This general format is intended to heighten awareness of writing strengths and weaknesses and to help teachers to recognise the great potential of pupils' writing if they wish to learn about individual pupils' abilities and difficulties.

Pupil's Assessment Sheet 1 is intended for teachers taking a general look at one of their own pupil's writing, either because the pupil concerned has only a few general writing difficulties that are easily discerned, or as a precursor to the more detailed analysis that will eventually be employed.

Pupil's Assessment Sheet 2 is limited for use when the assessment focuses on one aspect of writing. For example, when an area such as spelling is clearly the one where most difficulties lie. With this format, the area to be examined can be underlined to identify the aspect of writing to be examined at the outset.

Practitioners' real concern will be to apply these models to their own pupils' work. In this chapter, readers will be given an opportunity to practise the use of these models by examining a carefully chosen sample of pupils' writing. They will then be able to compare the extent to which their views concur with those of the author by referring to Appendix A (on page 114). A similar approach is used in successive chapters. Readers can then go to apply the techniques which they have learned, to their own situation.

The author's major objective is to ensure that pupils' written work is examined in the context of general writing tasks, also that, by one means or another, the standard of writing improves as pupils progress through their primary schools. It is not intended that the analyses of the examples included in this book should be exhaustive. For each, it would be possible to write a far more precise and extensive analysis - the book would also become very boring. Should readers draw different conclusions or begin to develop different criteria from those suggested here, this could well prove to be beneficial in the long run.

It is not possible to intervene with all of the children all of the time. However, by using this approach and its assessment format, children will also begin to enjoy and respond to the intervention process. To some extent, writing involves setting out on paper an aspect of oneself for all to see. Many pupils could do with an improvement in self-concept. This is one way in which it can be brought about.

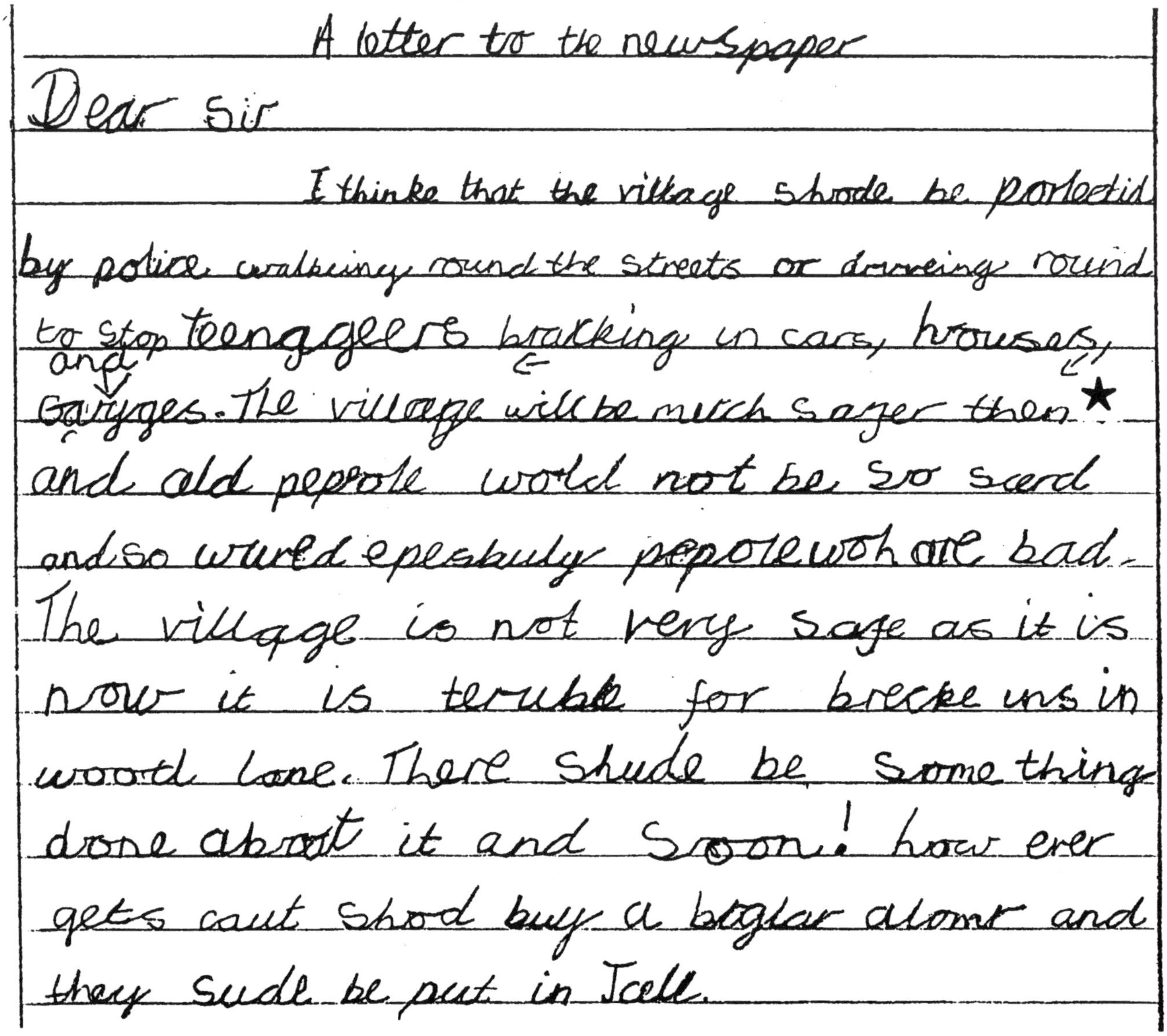

A letter to the newspaper

Dear Sir

I thinke that the village shode be portectid by police walkeing round the streets or drriveing round to stop teenaggeers braking in cars, houses, and garyges. The village will be much sager then ★ and old pepole world not be so scard and so wured epeshuly pepole who are bad. The village is not very sage as it is now it is terruble for brecke ins in woood lane. There shude be some thing done about it and Soon! how ever gets caut shod buy a biglar alomr and they sude be put in Jcell.

Figure 10 - Example of a letter written to a newspaper by a right-handed, 10 year old boy.

Assessing this sample of writing using the models given on pages 37, 38 and 39. Record what you think are his strengths, weaknesses and problems. Then set some teaching objectives for improving his general writing skills. Afterwards, refer to Appendix A on page 114 to see how far your conclusions concur with those of the author.

Assessing and Promoting Writing Skills

Teacher's Assessment Sheet

On the positive side:..

....

....

....

....

....

....

Problems occur in: ....

....

....

....

....

....

....

Teaching objectives in order of priority: ....

....

....

....

....

....

....

Assessing and Promoting Writing Skills

Pupil's Assessment Sheet 1

Name .... Class..

Date of writing task .... Time for completing writing task.............................

General writing characteristics

On the positive side: ....

....

....

....

....

....

Problems occur in: ....

....

....

....

....

....

Teaching objectives in order of priority: ....

....

....

....

....

....

Assessing and Promoting Writing Skills

Pupil's Assessment Sheet 2

Name ....Class..

Date of writing task ....Time for completing writing task.............................

Specific writing characteristics: Handwriting, Spelling, Punctuation, Grammar, Logical, stylistic and expressive aspects.
(underline as appropriate)

On the positive side:..

....

....

....

....

....

Problems occur in: ....

....

....

....

....

....

Teaching objectives in order of priority: ....

....

....

....

....

....

CHAPTER 9

Handwriting

National Curriculum requirements

Key Stage One Programme of Study states that pupils should be taught to hold a pencil comfortably in order to develop a legible style that follows the conventions of written English, including:

- writing from left to right and from top to bottom of the page;
- starting and finishing letters correctly;
- regularity of size and shape of letters;
- regularity of spacing of letters and words.

They should be taught the conventional ways of forming letters, both lower case and capitals.

They should build on their knowledge of letter formation to join letters in words. They should develop an awareness of the importance of clear and neat presentation in order to communicate their meaning effectively.

Key Stage Two Programme of Study states that pupils should be given opportunities to continue to develop legible handwriting in both joined up and printed styles. As pupils become increasingly competent and independent, they should be encouraged to develop greater control and fluency. They should be taught to use different forms of handwriting for different purposes, e.g. print for labelling maps or diagrams; a clear, neat hand for finished, presented work; a faster script for notes.

The most important aspect of learning to write is the proper formation of the 26 letters of the alphabet. The photocopiable letters, with starting points, shown in Appendix B can be used to help pupils with letter formation directionality. If these are formed correctly in the early stages, other aspects of handwriting develop almost automatically. For example, if an appropriate handwriting model is adopted, and if each letter finishes in the correct place, the pen or pencil will be automatically directed towards the beginning of the next letter.

There are numerous models on the educational market and a few are much better than others. I recommend either the P. Wallis Myers or the Christopher Jarman model, though this is not to say that a few others are not equally acceptable.

Writing from left to right

Children can be encouraged to write from left to right across the page by being given paper with panels of space in which to write. The paper can be A4 size and presented in the horizontal/landscape direction. Broad lines, perhaps two or three to the page are most helpful in the early stages. Pupils may not write on lines, in the first year or so, but may write between them, having some guidance that writing should go across the page. If the pupil has difficulty (a few will do mirror writing to begin with), put a star in the top left hand corner to show the starting place.

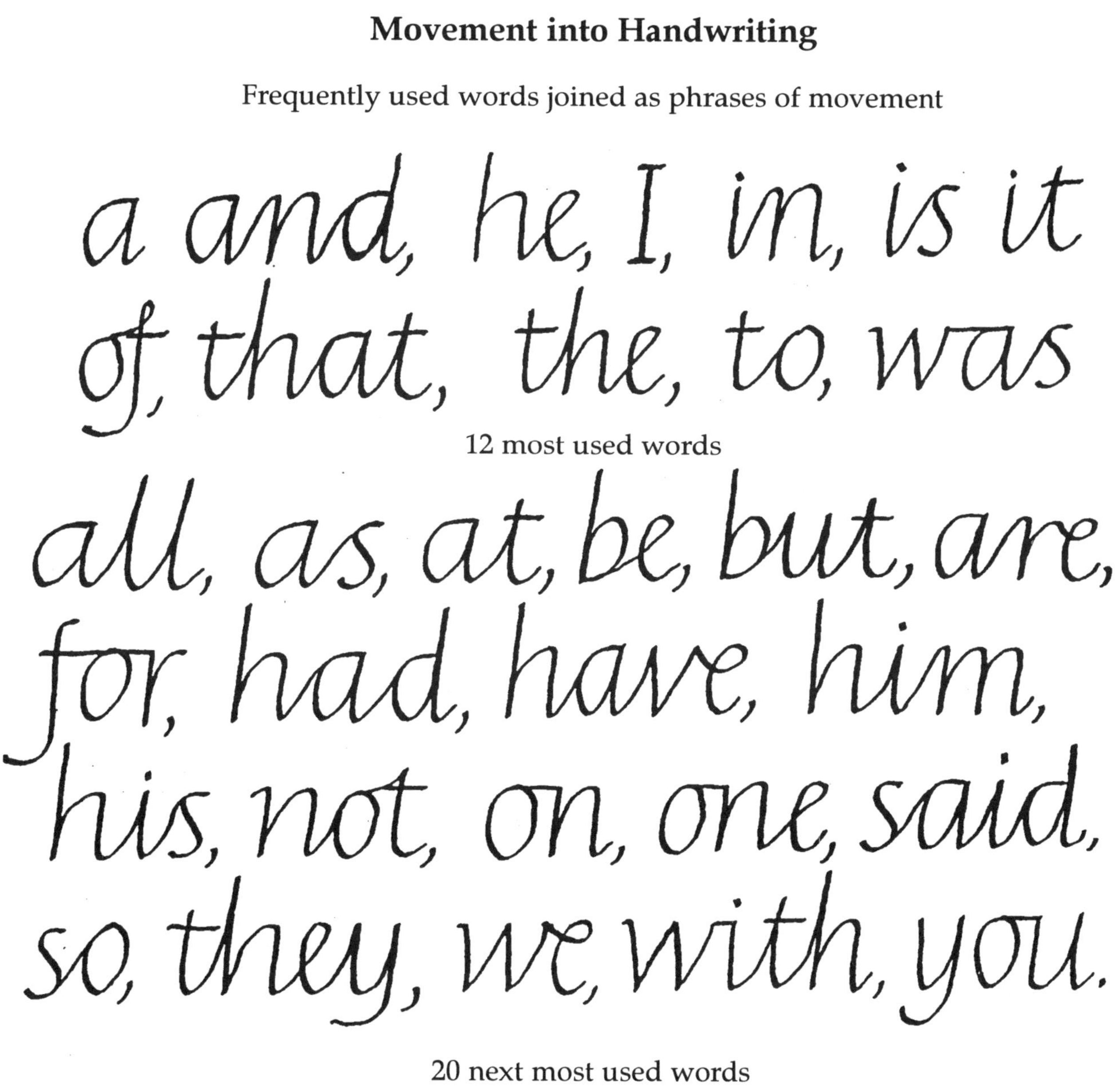

Figure 11 - The P. Wallis Myers 'Movement into Writing' model.

Regularity of size and shape of letters

Children can only be taught about relative letter size if they are introduced to lined paper. They need to understand the following concepts:

- The body of each letter sits on the writing baseline.
- The letters a c e i m n o r s u v w x z reach only to a writing midline.
- The letters g j p q y have parts which descend below the baseline.
- The letters b d f h k l t have parts which descend above the writing midline.

How to Join Letters

There are two kinds of join,

1. Horizontal,

wood top two on

vote from fox of

2. Diagonal,

main came do

his and mum in

The following letters are best left unjoined, as the pen ends up in an inconvenient position. Sometimes however, a loop may be made if desired.

b g j p q y s

Figure 12 - The Christopher Jarman model.

If pupils are introduced to lined paper in Reception class, there should be a variety of wide lined formats, so that letters are not constricted as pupils write. It is useful to draw in an extra line for the upper level of midline letters, or use three of four parallel-lined paper, from time to time. If pupils do not know that letters have different sizes, they cannot be expected to make different sizes when they write them. Appendix C has examples of heavy lined and four-lined paper formats which can be useful at different stages of handwriting development. Other lined formats can be made available in school and used for individual children who require them.

When relative letter size is not developed at Reception class level, irregularity persists into the upper junior and secondary school. When this occurs, the following procedure will help:

- estimate the natural size of the writer's midline letters;
- draw in an extra line between the normal lines of the exercise book or line writing paper;
- show the pupil how this will help him or her to regularise the different sizes of letter parts.

Regularity of spacing between words

When pupils recognise and use different letter sizes the spacing problems, so often seen in young children's writing, may not occur. It seems as if those helped with vertical size for letters can manage the word spacing much better than we expect. However, if inordinately small spacing persists, a cardboard finger can be provided until spacing is regularised. The extra wide spacing shown by some pupils, and by left handers in particular, should also disappear as writers are helped with alignment and as the writing of words becomes more competent.

Rules for joining letters

Although correct letter formation helps considerably when joining is begun, a few rules will help to make sure that joins are the most economical, and that they lead to a fast and fluent style:

- Letters which finish at the bottom join diagonally to the next letter:

  a c d e g h i j k l m n qu t u y z

  (When letters have become well formed, y, g, and j can be looped)

- Letters which finish at the top join horizontally to the next letter:

  o r v w

- Some letters which follow others will need an 'over and back' join from the previous letter:

  a c d g o qu

  These joins occur in words like: cat, sat, no, dog, back.

Ask the pupils to write the following words if you wish to check letter joins:

the and from girl

These four words contain most of the joins required.

Readers are invited to use the assessment/teaching models on pages 37, 38 and 39 when making their own attempts at assessing the example of handwriting shown in *Figure 13*.

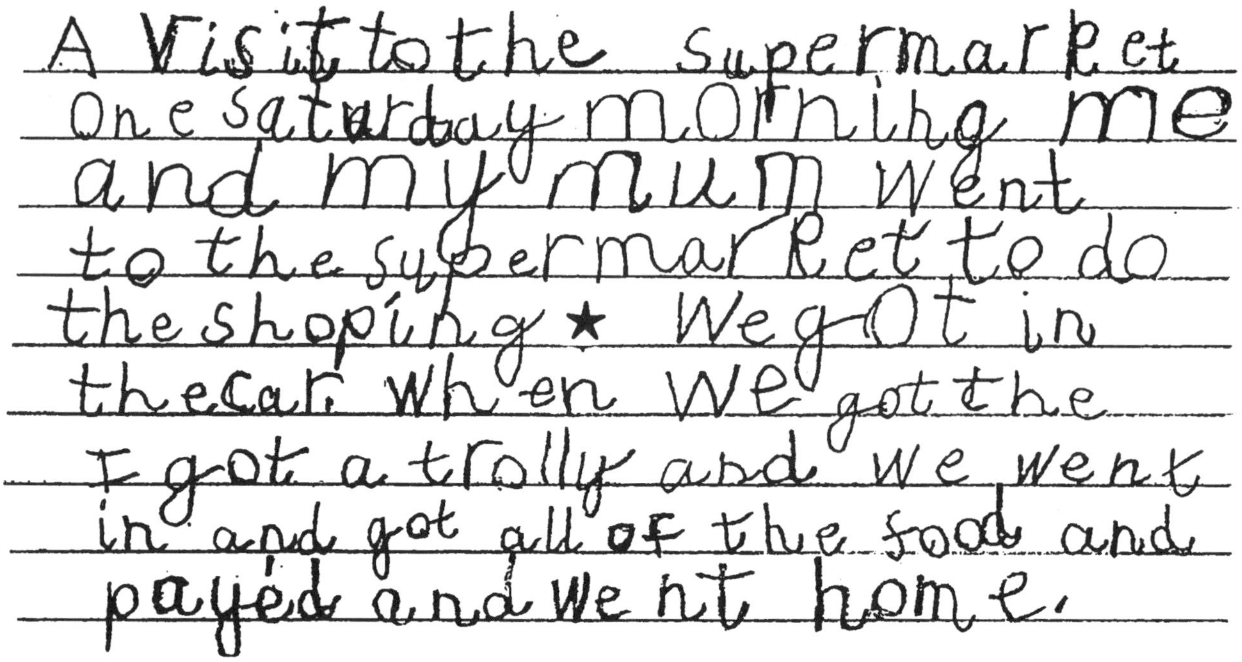

A visit to the supermarket
One saturday morning me
and my mum went
to the supermarket to do
the shoping ★ We got in
the car. when we got the
I got a trolly and we went
in and got all of the food and
payed and went home.

Figure 13 - The writing of a right handed boy, aged 8 years 10 months, is assessed for handwriting.

Guidance for the assessment of the writing in Figure 13

On the positive side:

- the majority of letters seem to be properly formed and begin at the correct entry points;
- pencil strokes are relatively firm, indicating that motor control is adequate and that handwriting need not be a major problem.

Problems occur in:

- the formation of letter 'o' which often has the entry point near to the writing baseline;
- inconsistent letter sizes;
- inconsistent word spacing;
- inconsistent letter spacing.

Teaching objectives in order of priority might be:

- all small letters should begin at the top, except 'd' and 'e'. Ensure that the letter 'o' and all other letters begin at the correct entry points;

- show how the penultimate line of writing has relatively appropriate letter sizes. Draw pencil lines at the appropriate 'x' height for his next piece of writing, to encourage different heights for 'x' height and ascending letters;

  Examples: a c e i m n o r s u v w x z
  b d h k l

- spacing may improve spontaneously as letter sizes become more consistent. If it does not do so, strategies for teaching spacing should follow. For example, make a cardboard finger to place after each word is written and before the next word begins.

CHAPTER 10

Spelling

National Curriculum requirements

Key Stage One Programme of Study states that pupils should be taught to:

- write each letter of the alphabet;
- use their knowledge of sound-symbol relationships and phonological patterns;
- recognise and use simple spelling patterns;
- write common letter strings within familiar and common words;
- spell commonly occurring simple words;
- spell words with common prefixes and suffixes.

Pupils should be taught to check the accuracy of their spelling, and to use word books and dictionaries, identifying initial letters as the means of locating words. They should be given opportunities to experiment with the spelling of complex words and to discuss misapplied generalisations and other reasons for misspellings. Close attention should be paid to word families.

Key Stage Two Programme of Study states that pupils should be accumulating a bank of words that they can spell correctly, and should be taught to check spellings and meanings of words, using dictionaries where appropriate. When looking up words, pupils should be taught to apply their knowledge of initial and subsequent letters and the organisation of dictionaries, including headings, abbreviations and other conventions. They should be taught:

- the meaning, use, and spelling of common prefixes and suffixes;
- the relevance of word families, roots and origins of words;
- alternative ways of writing the same sound;
- the spelling of words with inflectional endings.

Pupils should be taught to:

- spell complex, polysyllabic words that conform to regular patterns, and to break long and complex words into more manageable units, by using their knowledge of meaning and word structure;
- memorise the visual patterns of words, including those that are irregular;
- recognise silent letters;

- use the apostrophe to spell shortened forms of words;
- use appropriate terminology, including vowel and consonant.

A Spelling Programme

The spelling programme presented here is arranged in the following sequence:

A. mastering 26 letters of the alphabet;

B. writing monosyllabic words;

C. writing 'Key Words';

D. differentiating between vowels and consonants;

E. understanding short and long vowel sounds;

F. learning about syllables;

G. knowing and recognising major syllable groups;

H. using the apostrophe;

I. recognising base/root words;

J. learning about prefixes;

K. learning about suffixes;

L. learning to spell through word meanings.

Items **A** to **L** will now be dealt with in that sequence.

A. Inevitably, the bedrock of literacy is the alphabet. There are only 26 letters, each of which has sound, name, and directional form. A complete and automatic mastery of the alphabet is an essential foundation for all pupils. It should be a major objective for all Reception to Year 2 children. An easy way of assessing and teaching letter forms is by use of a set of cards which have letter on one side and letter and picture clue on the other (Alston 1994). Photocopiable masters for making these cards are presented in Appendix B.
B. The letters are taught one by one, with picture clue to help those with difficulties. Children quickly learn letter sounds when the letter only is shown and the card turned to reveal the picture clue when the child falters. The child learns letter directionality by tracing the letter from the starting point. When writing is established, letter directionality can be assessed, at any stage, as follows:

1. Present a letter card.
2. Ask about sound (and eventually name).

3. Cover the card.
4. Pupil writes the letter in a cell of the grid.
5. Teacher observes whether the letter is formed correctly and notes details of movement errors.

Capitals can also be assessed in this way but pupils tend to have less difficulty with capitals - they can be taught when lower case letters are established. It is important to teach or revise capital letters and their functions when pupils are writing at the level of the average seven-year-old. Children often need reminding about sentence beginnings. They find it hard to differentiate proper nouns which need a capital letter and the names of things that are important to them, such as brother and birthday which do not need a capital letter.

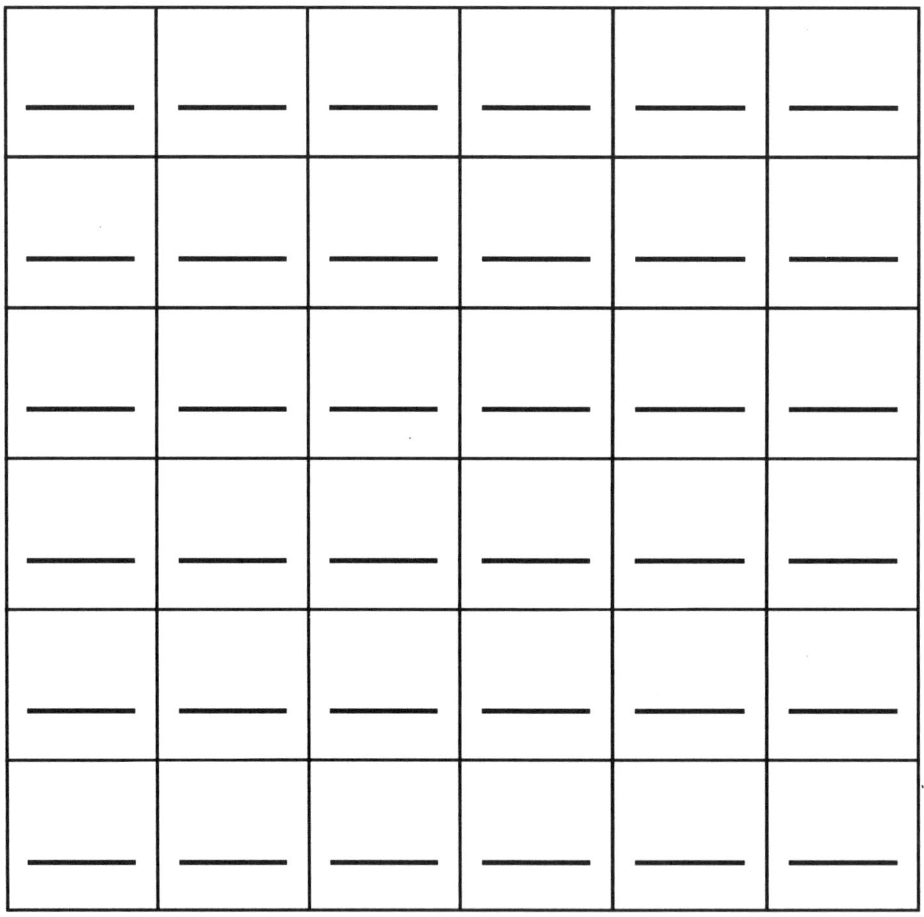

Figure 14 - A grid for assessing letter directionality.

B. The teaching of individual letter sounds goes hand-in-hand with writing simple words. Known letter sounds help the child to build simple monosyllabic words; a foundation for writing and spelling performance. The monosyllabic words 'cat' 'and' 'is' 'not' all require knowledge of consonants and simple vowel sounds. Given the tools of letter sounds and pencil and paper, the child can spontaneously attempt the words he or she wishes to write.

C. 'Key words' *(Figure 15)* are the words most commonly used for reading and writing. They can be taught so that the written vocabulary word bank can be extended. Twelve words occur so frequently that they account for a quarter of the words we write. About 100 words account for half the words we write. Pupils can be told about Key Words, which can be given on a wall poster, on a card on each child's desk, or in a similar manner. The first 12 words can be gradually extended to help each child to build a written word bank. The child's personal words complete the ongoing word bank record.

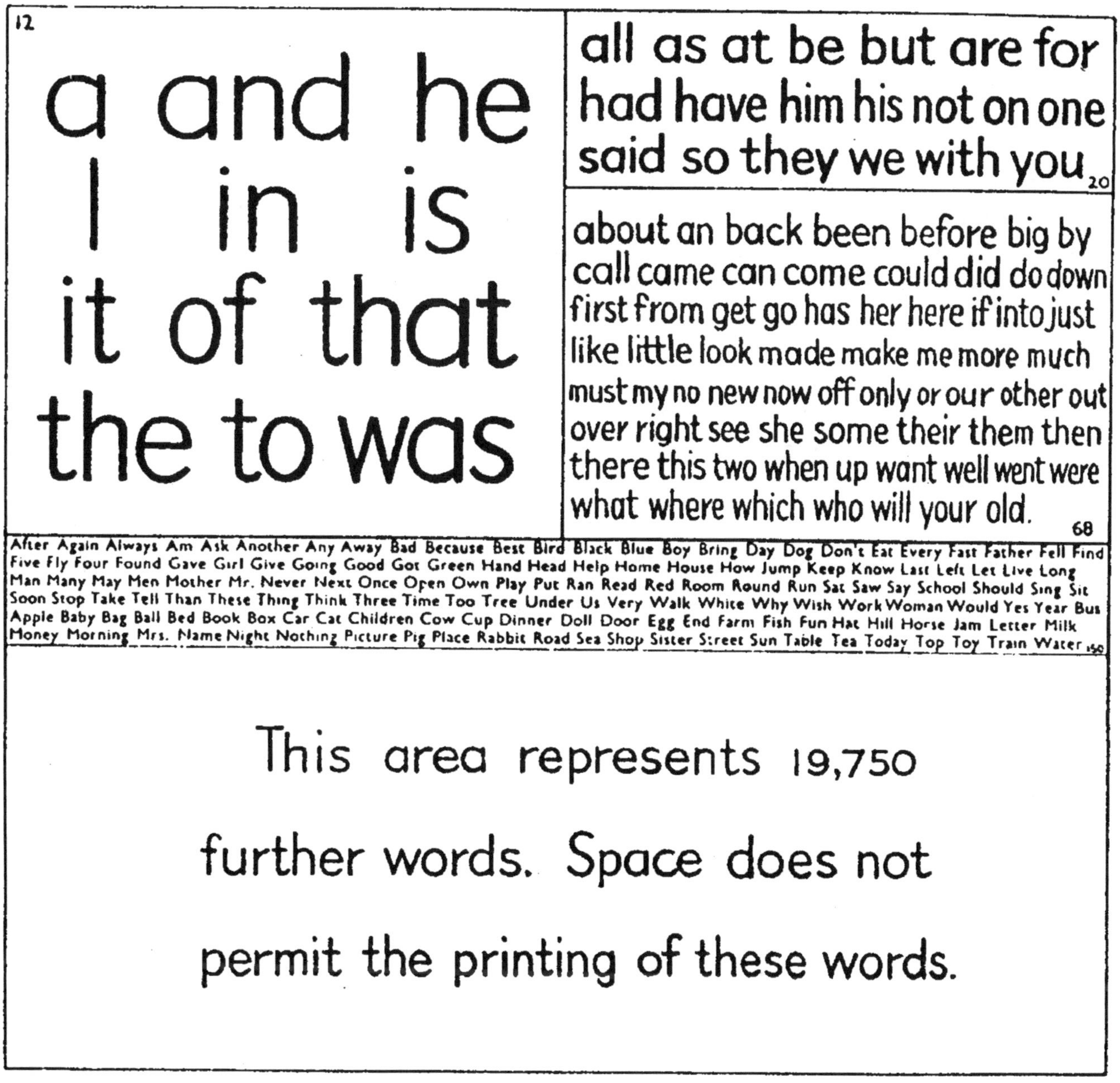

Figure 15 - Key words can be used to establish a working vocabulary for spelling.
This proportional representation of Key Words to Literacy (McNally, J., Murray, W. 1968; Murray, W. 1991) shows most of the used words in English as applied to the vocabulary of an average adult. (McNally, J., Murray, W. 1962).

D. Vowels are used frequently, one or more in each syllable/separate unit within a word:

a e i o u

The other 21 letters are called consonants:

b c d f g h j k l m n p q r s t v w x y z

A sheet for recording knowledge of sounds and names is easily constructed:

	b	c	d	f	g	h	j	k	l	m	n	p	q	r	s	t	v	w	x	y	z
sound	_	_	_	_	_	_	_	_	_	_	_	_	_	_	_	_	_	_	_	_	_
name	_	_	_	_	_	_	_	_	_	_	_	_	_	_	_	_	_	_	_	_	_

E. Vowels are important letters. There is one or more in each syllable that we speak or write. Vowels can make long or short sounds. They greatly influence the way in which words are spelt. As soon as pupils are ready, e.g. at reading level 6½ years, it is helpful to show marks that differentiate long and short vowels:

as in:	ă cat	ĕ egg	ĭ pin	ŏ log	ŭ run
as in:	ā cake	ē be	ī like	ō no	ū mule

F. Syllables are word 'beats' and can be illustrated in that way, teacher and pupils beating out word syllables in spare moments during the day. Pupils should be able to tell how many syllables each word has.

Examples:

Word	*Number of beats*	*Syllables*
me	one beat	one
himself	two beats	two
inventive	three beats	three
inconsistent	four beats	four

Many writers miss out syllables when writing, for example:

Omitted syllable word	*Correct word*
intest	interest
tevision	television

G. A knowledge of six important syllable groups helps pupils to divide up words in a meaningful manner:

1. **Closed syllables** have a vowel-consonant structure. The vowel is 'shut in' by the final consonant/consonants. The vowel says its short sound.
   These words show examples of closed syllables:
   man cat then egg pit sit on top up sun

2. **Open syllables** have a vowel at the end. There is no end consonant to close the vowel in. The vowel usually says its name.
   These words show examples of open syllables:
   he go me so hel/lo be/have pu/pil

3. **Vowel-Consonant-e syllables** are found at the ends of words. The final e is silent. The vowel before the consonant says its name.
   These words show examples of vowel-consonant-e syllables:
   came late fine kite fume tube

4. **Diphthong syllables** have two vowels together that make only one sound. The sound is most often the name of the first vowel, but sometimes the first vowel says its common sound. The second vowel is silent.
   These words show examples of diphthong syllables:
   rain been mean flies goes

5. **Consonant-l-e syllables** come at the end of a word and end with a silent 'e'.
   These words show examples of consonant-l-e syllables:
   able apple topple ripple rabble puzzle

6. **Syllables with vowel-r** show that all vowels can be followed by 'r' and the sounds made by the syllables are variable.
   These are words showing vowel-r syllables:
   farm term birth torn churn

H. The apostrophe is used for two purposes:

1. It shows that someone owns something, as in:
   Jane's book
   Peter's football
   The dog's collar
   My Mum's car

   If the noun is plural, the apostrophe comes after the plural form of the name, as in:
   boys' football team
   men's hockey team
   girls' classroom
   women's swimming cubicles

2. It shows where a letter or letters have been missed out, as in:

it is	it's
I have	I've
do not	don't
they are	they're
can not	can't
was not	wasn't
there is	there's
you are	you're

I. Base elements are the same in words with related meanings. They can sometimes be base/root words. For example:

'sign' is the base element for:	signature signal resign design
'ear' is the base element for:	hear heard ear-ring
'you' is the base element for:	your yours yourself

(Ramsden, 1993a, p 45)

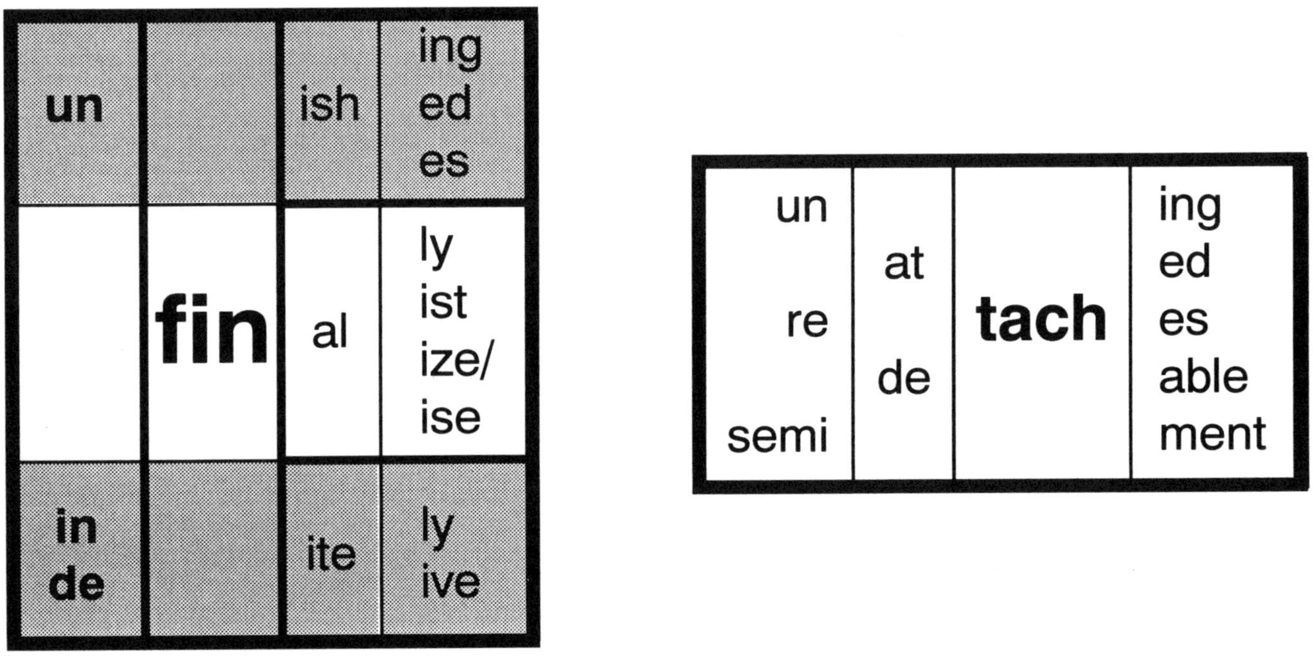

Figure 16 - Word Matrices, showing how words can be built from different elements of meaning, including base element, prefix, word ending and suffix (Ramsden, *Getting it Write,* page 36).

J. A prefix occurs before the base/root word and affects meaning.
For example:

- the word 'born' is changed by adding 'un' - to make 'unborn';
- the word 'trust' is changed by adding 'mis' - to make 'mistrust'.

(Ramsden, 1993a, pp 47-53)

A complete list of prefixes is presented in Ramsden (1993a), page 53.

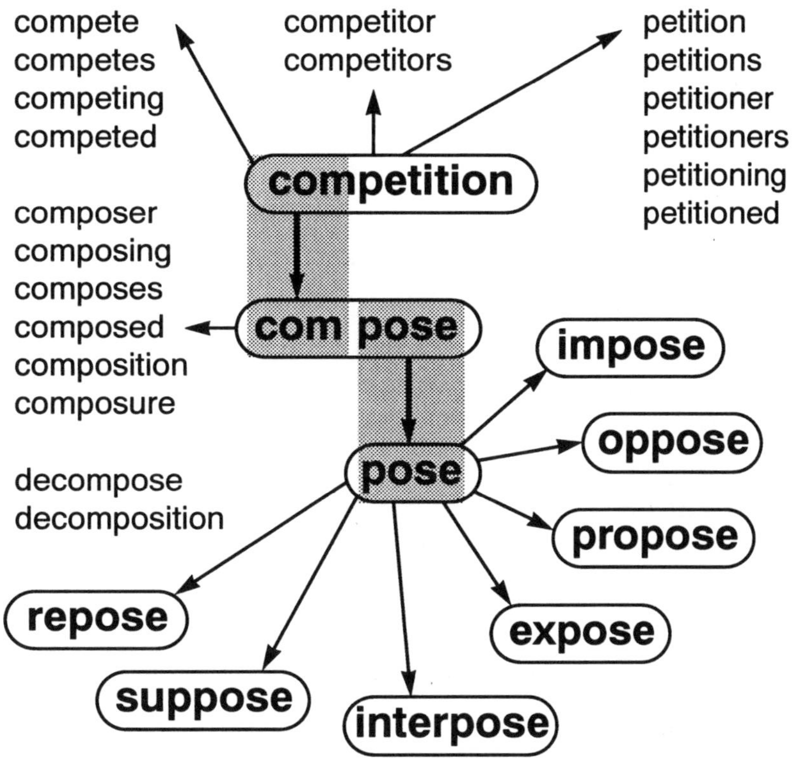

Figure 17 - A word web, useful for teaching spelling through meaning (Ramsden, Rescuing Spelling, page 97).

K. A suffix is added after the base/root and affects meaning.
For example:

- the word 'king' is changed by adding 'dom' - to make 'kingdom';
- the word 'brother' is changed by adding 'hood' - to make 'brotherhood'.

(Ramsden, 1993a. pp 48-49)

Morphology

The term 'morphology' refers to meaning, in this case to the meaning of words. Ramsden makes an excellent case for teaching spelling almost totally through meanings, showing that all our words have their origins and associations, and the way we spell can be traced back to them.

Words from old English refer to basic materials, objects and ideas (life was relatively simple in those days). Old English words include:

igh	sigh, thigh, high
wh	who, where, what
aw, ow, ew	raw, blow, blew

Many of our words show their Latinate origins:

Some end with 'us', the plural of which is 'i'

cactus	cacti

Or they end with 'um', the plural of which is 'a'

medium	media
stadium	stadia

Greek influences occur in:

'tele' for television and telescope;

'poly' for polygon and polytechnic.

Modern French imports include:

chalet crochet chauffeur chef brochure

Ramsden informs us that with full knowledge of word origins, i.e. etymology, the spelling of all words will be logical, i.e. there do not need to be spelling exceptions. For those wishing to extend their knowledge or words, origins, and their relationship to other words, a reliable and comprehensive dictionary is the best source.

Identifying spelling weaknesses

When children have begun to write relatively freely, it is possible to identify the group to which, as spellers, they are likely to belong. Torbe (1977) drew our attention to a way of classifying spellers. First, there are those who make only occasional errors, i.e. those who will progress with help only when they need it. He referred also to three types of spelling problems:

1. *Visual memory difficulties*
   Writers don't remember what the word look like:

   'please' may be written as 'plees'

   'field' may be written as 'fyld'

2. *Auditory memory/sequencing difficulties*
   These writers try to remember what the word looks like, but THEY DO NOT SAY THE WORD BEFORE THEY WRITE IT.

   'girl' may be written as 'glri'

   'table' may be written as 'tble'

3. *Weak SOUND to SYMBOL relationship*
   These pupils have both visual and auditory memory difficulties and are left with virtually no strategies for spelling:

   'television' may be written as 'taviru'

   'girl' may be written as 'lrg'

(Torbe 1977; Alston, 1992, 1994)

Introducing spelling strategies

When pupil weaknesses have been identified, strategies for overcoming them must be introduced. A strategy advocated by Peters, and publicised by Cripps, **'LOOK-COVER-WRITE-CHECK'** has become very popular, particularly in primary education. The very introduction of a strategy has been instrumental in raising spelling standards for many pupils. The LOOK-COVER-WRITE-CHECK approach has been helpful to pupils showing weak visual memory. They have been able to employ and supplement it by their own strategy of 'auditory/phonic attack'. Cripps now suggests a strategy of LOOK-SAY-COVER-WRITE-CHECK, which should be helpful to a wider range of pupils than his earlier approach.

Those with auditory memory and sequencing difficulties are unlikely to succeed with LOOK-COVER-WRITE-CHECK, or even from LOOK-SAY-COVER-WRITE-CHECK. However, saying the word as part of the strategy is helpful to all pupils. For these spellers and for those with even greater problems, a SOUND/SYMBOL approach is more likely to succeed.

When pupils have begun to write, though perhaps imperfectly, the teacher will be able to identify spelling weaknesses. Pupils may by this time be $6^1/_2$ to 7 years of age and can be treated as relatively mature writers. In this situation, alphabet names are the most helpful, and will complement the multisensory approach I advocate. I suggest:

- **Say** the word.

- **Write** the word (using the dictionary or adult to help).

- **Look** at the word.

- **Spell** out the word saying letter names.

- **Cover** the word.

- **Say** the word.

- **Write** the word, saying each letter name as it is written.

- **Check** the word.

If there is a bit of a word that is more difficult, write over those letters in the incorrect word, i.e. write correct letters over the incorrect ones.

Aids for this strategy, which should always be available and used, are:

- an easy to use dictionary (some have the target word in colour);
- pieces of paper 4cms x 6cms - to practice words;
- voice;
- eyes;
- ears;
- handwriting - using a joined script.

Strategies for learning to spell can be used as different parts of the spelling syllabus are being taught, e.g. during the teaching of Key Words, syllables, or base elements.

Ramsden's spelling strategies can be built when the speller can adopt a mature approach to words. Pupils can be encouraged to question word origins and similarities.

Ramsden advises us to:

Segment words, using meaning as the first means of analysis so that:

lovely	becomes	love - ly
wanting	becomes	want - ing
understand	becomes	under - stand

Understanding the term 'graph' allows the analysis:

photo	**graph**	y
para		ic al y
geo		er
tele		
auto		s

A number of combinations from the above words allow us to spell correctly through segmenting and word meanings.

'Prefix - base word - suffix' is a common structure, so that 'unsightly' can be separated to its basic elements:

PREFIX	BASE WORD	SUFFIX
un	sight	ly

(Ramsden, 1993a, pp 45-51)

Recent research

More recent research from the NZCER (Croft, 1983) has pursued an even more thorough analysis of spelling standards and teaching approaches. He concluded that less-able spellers in particular, benefited from more structured word study programmes. As well as a basic core vocabulary, the 1983 lists included words that children need for different aspects of writing or for different areas of the curriculum, for example, place names (airport, market); body parts (bone, blood); food (bread, cake), and other similar and useful short vocabulary lists. A further list of *Commonly Misspelt Words* is presented here *(Figure 18)*, with Croft's reminder that words in this list may continue to be misspelt throughout the primary school years. As in earlier publications, the New Zealanders advocate reliable multisensory approaches for the teaching of spelling.

Croft's guideline, *Combining Spelling with Writing in Primary Classrooms* (NZCER 1992), includes the 300 most often used words from a national sample of New Zealand primary school children's writing. For our purpose, it is interesting to note that there is considerable concordance between the first 40 or so New Zealand words and those identified by McNally and Murray. After that stage, a few words such as 'people', 'started' and 'around' reflect the writing rather than reading vocabulary needs of young children. Croft's statistics give a salutary reminder that the word 'the' by itself accounts for six per cent of all words written, and 'the', 'and', 'I', 'to', 'a', 'was', 'we', 'it', 'in' and 'of' account for just one quarter of written words.

aeroplane	different	later	scared
allowed	disappeared	lot	someone
arrived	doesn't	met	spare
beautiful	everyone	minute	started
believe	everything	myself	stopped
board	everywhere	nearly	straight
boat	favourite	nice	suddenly
bought	finally	noise	swimming
broke	frightened	opened	things
brother	front	outside	threw
buy	guard	passed	tired
cannot	happened	piece	turned
caught	hiding	police	upstairs
clothes	hospital	present	usually
coming	hungry	ready	we're
course	hurt	really	whole
decided	inside	remembered	without
didn't	kept	running	you're

Figure 18 - Commonly Misspelt Words (Croft, C., NZCER, 1983)

Using the assessment/teaching models on pages 37, 38 and 39, readers are again invited to assess the sample of writing in *Figure 19,* paying particular attention to the writer's spelling.

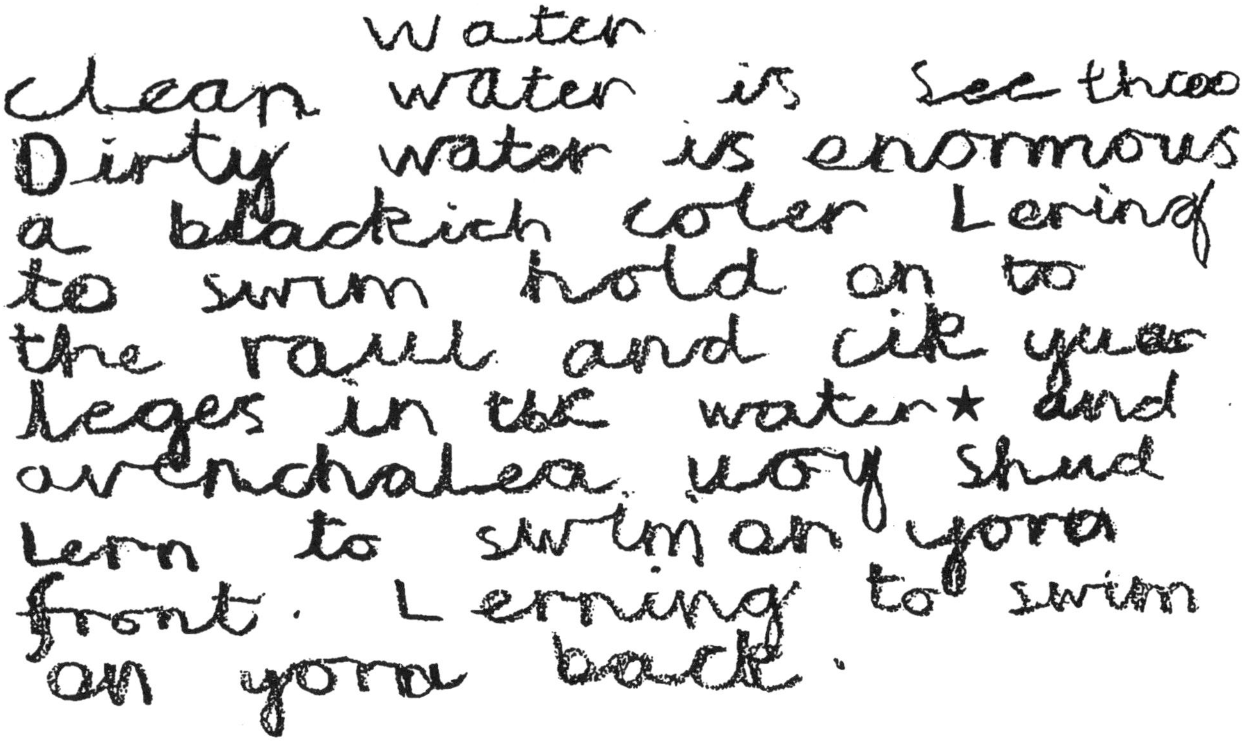

Figure 19 - Sample of writing from a right-handed boy, aged 9 years 5 months.

Guidance for the assessment of spelling in Figure 19

On the positive side:

- The impression is given that the writer enjoys writing and has something to write about.
- He may have been helped with words in the first sentence and spells many of them correctly.
- He is prepared to tackle big words, e.g. 'eventually/avenchalea'.

Problems occur in:

- the deterioration of spelling as the script progresses;
- his phonic approach to spelling, i.e. he attempts to write most words as they sound;
- inaccurate sequence of letters in some words, so that:
  'your' is written as 'yuor' or 'yoru';
  'you' is written as 'uoy';
- the use of c and k alone in 'cik'.

Teaching objectives in order of priority might be:

- for simpler 'Key Words', he should use the Look-Cover-Write-Check approach for learning spelling, in order to strengthen his visual perception of letter configurations;
- the incorporation of a multi-sensory sound/element for longer and more difficult words will give further security to spelling ability. When learning new words he should:

  - Write the word correctly (using a dictionary or teacher to help him).
  - Say the word clearly.
  - Write the word, **naming** each letter as he writes it.
  - Cover the word.
  - Write the word, **naming** each letter as he writes it.
  - Check the word.
  - Say the word clearly.

- this procedure can be used for several weeks so that certain elements of it will be automatically incorporated into his learning style;
- he should follow a 'Key Word' spelling programme.

CHAPTER 11

Punctuation

National Curriculum requirements

Key Stage One Programme of Study states that pupils should be taught that punctuation is essential to help a reader understand what is written. Pupils should be given opportunities to read their work aloud in order to understand the connections between the punctuation of a sentence and intonation and emphasis. Pupils should be taught to punctuate their writing, be consistent in their use of capital letters, full stops and question marks, and begin to use commas.

Key Stage Two Programme of Study states that pupils should be taught to use punctuation marks correctly in their writing, including full stops, question and exclamation marks, commas, inverted commas, and apostrophes to mark possession.

Learning to use punctuation is often difficult for young writers because accurate usage requires an awareness of a number of concepts which are not easily understood. Often it will be apparent from their actual writing whether or not writers are ready to use particular punctuation conventions. For example, if they clearly write in sentences with regard to meaning, but do not use capital letters and full stops, then they are ready to be taught this convention.

Although the National Curriculum requirements refer to the connection between the punctuation of a sentence and intonation and emphasis, we do not often encourage writers to read aloud so that they will hear where punctuation marks should occur in their own writing. Our young and/or less able writers are unable to understand punctuation if they read only to themselves. Reading aloud for young writers will greatly aid the development of punctuation. Could there be a time in every writing lesson, when each pupil reads to his neighbour and in turn listens to what his neighbour has written?

Sentences

The following features are important:

- Does he or she write in sentences with regard to meaning?
- Does he or she punctuate with capital letters?
- Does he or she use full stops?
- Does he or she use capital letters for sentence beginnings?
- Does he or she understand proper nouns and use capital letters for them?
- Is there use of: question marks, exclamation marks, inverted commas for direct speech, apostrophes for possession and apostrophes for omission?
- Does he or she use commas: - to separate items in a list?
- for reading/writing pauses?
- for dividing off a clause?

- Are brackets used as a diversion from the main point of the text?
- Are brackets used to present interesting information not essential to the sequence of the script?
- Are pairs of dashes used to enclose information which may not be essential to the main script?

Paragraphs

Many pupils, even at the age of 11 years and older, do not divide free written work into paragraphs. Many will not know why we have the convention of dividing narrative in this way. Even literate adults can be uncertain of where a new paragraph should begin. However, a close look at some pupils' work will show that what they write is actually written in clusters of meaning, i.e. in natural paragraphs which are not formally divided on the written page. When they read their writing aloud, they may well pause longer when a new chunk of information is begun. If not, they can be taught to do so.

Teaching children about paragraphs is a way of teaching them to organise their writing. For example, if they are writing about a person, in the first paragraph it might be a good idea to tell readers who the person is and/or what he or she looks like. The next paragraph could then describe why he or she is such a special person. The final paragraph might indicate the relationship between the special person and the writer, what activities they pursue together, and so on. This kind of approach not only helps writers to organise their work but may also suggest how the writing can be extended through use of adjectival phrases, and so forth.

Using the now familiar assessment/teaching models on page 37, 38 and 39 readers are invited to assess the sample of writing in *Figure 20,* with punctuation in mind.

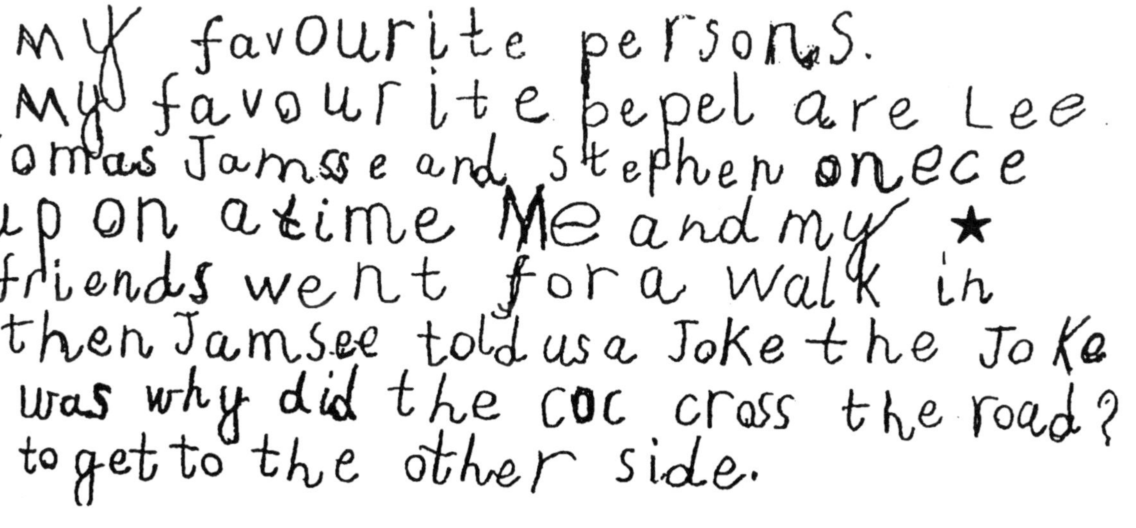
My favourite persons.
My favourite pepel are Lee
Tomas Jamse and Stephen onece
upon atime Me and my ★
friends went for a walk in
then Jamsee told us a Joke the JoKe
was why did the coc cross the road?
to get to the other side.

Figure 20 - A sample of written work from a right handed boy, aged 8 years 10 months.

Guidance for the assessment of Figure 13 for punctuation

On the positive side:

- A full stop is used in the title, though inappropriately;

- it indicates that the writer knows about full stops;
- a full stop is used at the end of the writing;
- a question mark is placed after the question.

Problems occur in:

- the absence of full stop after 'Stephen' and after 'Joke';
- the absence of capital letters to begin sentences at: 'Once...' 'The joke...';
- the absence of commas;
- the absence of inverted commas for the question and for the answer.

Teaching objectives in order of priority might be:

- Use sentences he has already written to teach capital letters and full stops as appropriate. (Write each sentence on a strip of paper to emphasises what sentence indicates. Put the sentence papers together to make a paragraph.)
- Show how the question and answer are special kinds of sentences, and that inverted commas can be placed at the beginning and ends of speech elements.
- Eventually, show how different parts of the script can be extended, e.g. by writing more about Thomas, James and Stephen. Extended sections can then be separated into paragraphs.

CHAPTER 12

Grammatical Features of Writing

National Curriculum requirements

Key Stage One Programme of Study states that pupils should be introduced to the vocabulary, grammar and structures of written standard English, including subject-verb agreement, and the use of the verb 'to be' in past and present tenses. They should be taught to apply their existing linguistic knowledge, drawn from oral language and their experience of reading, to develop their understanding of the sentences and how word choice and order are crucial to clarity of meaning.

Key Stage Two Programme of Study states that pupils should be given opportunities to develop their understanding of the grammar of complex sentences, including clauses and phrases. They should be taught how to use paragraphs, linking sentences together coherently. They should be taught to use the standard written forms of nouns, pronouns, verbs, adjectives, adverbs, prepositions, conjunctions and verb tenses.

As the National Curriculum Attainment Target suggests, the aim is to ensure that pupils have the ability to use different forms of grammatical structure as they are required; in this way, they can become proficient and versatile writers.

Pupils who have difficulty with writing may also have experienced spoken language difficulties. Spoken language structures which are not well established, cannot be employed automatically, and are unlikely to be transferred easily into the written idiom. Writing, in these circumstances, remains at a simple level, dependent upon surface description, rather than upon objective reporting of people, objects, and/or events in different dimensions of experience. A competent use of verb forms is required for more advanced objective writing.

There are some grammatical errors which occur so frequently that they are worthy of attention. Some pupils seem to use them during most of their primary school days, yet attention at an appropriate stage could help pupils to abandon them in favour of the correct written forms. National Curriculum requirements draw attention to the frequent incorrect association of subject and verb using the verb 'to be'. The combinations 'we was' and 'you was' are common even in adult language; those who speak in this way will inevitably transfer those errors to writing. Past tense of verbs such as 'buyed' for 'bought' and 'writ' for 'wrote' are also heard relatively often.

In writing, there are other errors which occur frequently enough to warrant special attention. The verb 'to have', for example, can be hazardous for many pupils, and:

'you hafd to'
'he hadt to'
'he should of'

are common features in less able pupils' writing. The past tenses of many verbs provide pitfalls for many immature speakers and writers. For example, 'buyed' is used instead of 'bought', and 'keeped' instead of 'kept'. 'Much' and 'many' are common sources of confusion, so that questions like:

'How much cars did he have?'
or
'How much days is it to Christmas'.

are commonly encountered in classrooms. Older pupils, and many adults let themselves down by errors in the use of adjectives of comparison. Use of the comparitive form unnecessarily or inappropriately, such as,

'much betterer than'
'more happier'
or
'more quieter than'

reminds us that confusions such as these could have been resolved at primary school level. Making sure of noun - verb concordance is particularly important.

Because language is complex, it is not possible or profitable to write more extensively about the structures which pupils do or should employ. However, some of the major teaching point might be as follows:

- Does the writer differentiate between proper nouns and common nouns?

- Are phrases such as noun phrases very simple or expanded ones:

  e.g. Can 'the boy' be extended to 'the big red haired boy'?

- Are common verb tenses, regular and irregular, commonly understand and utilised?

- Are differences shown between direct and indirect speech:

  Direct Speech
  The boy said, 'I am going to London.'

  Indirect Speech
  The boy said that he was going to London.

- Is there correct and consistent use of pronouns:

  I, him, her, it, one?

- Is there appropriate use of connectives:

  and, then, but, when, after, so, because?

- Are correct verb tenses employed:

  e.g. jumps, is jumping, jumped, was jumping, had jumped, will jump?

Try assessing *Figure 21* from a grammatical point of view using the assessment/teaching model on pages 37, 38 and 39 for your own attempt.

our Village

our Village is a place were thir are menny krickent clubs and thir are not much Shop in this Village and our Village is quit Big for Live in and ther are Lots of houses ther is a club for adults not for children thir is a good scool acros from the club and we Like at school thir is now Litir in the Shool yard I Like my villey thir is a hoke club for children and a playe sceame for Little Babes and thir is only one Shop in the village and I am warting about Wood Lane thir is a play field for people take dogs walke every day. ther are the wooods that is a big place for dogs and children play down one a dog got stok in this Big hole and thir are park in Wood Lane

thir is now man road Becouse thear is not much cars in this Little well quit Big villay and all people drop all of the Litter and I used to pick ~~it~~ it up and frow it in the Bin thir is mesira and this is a Lit Bit Bigger Becouse thir are more cars thir are some caredes round the Back off my hose were cars park and thir Bighall end and that got more shops than were I Like in the carrage-road the carriges are lots of glass and ther are a Big pile of flats thir is a libry in Bignal end past and thir is now bin around Wood Lane thir is no smashed

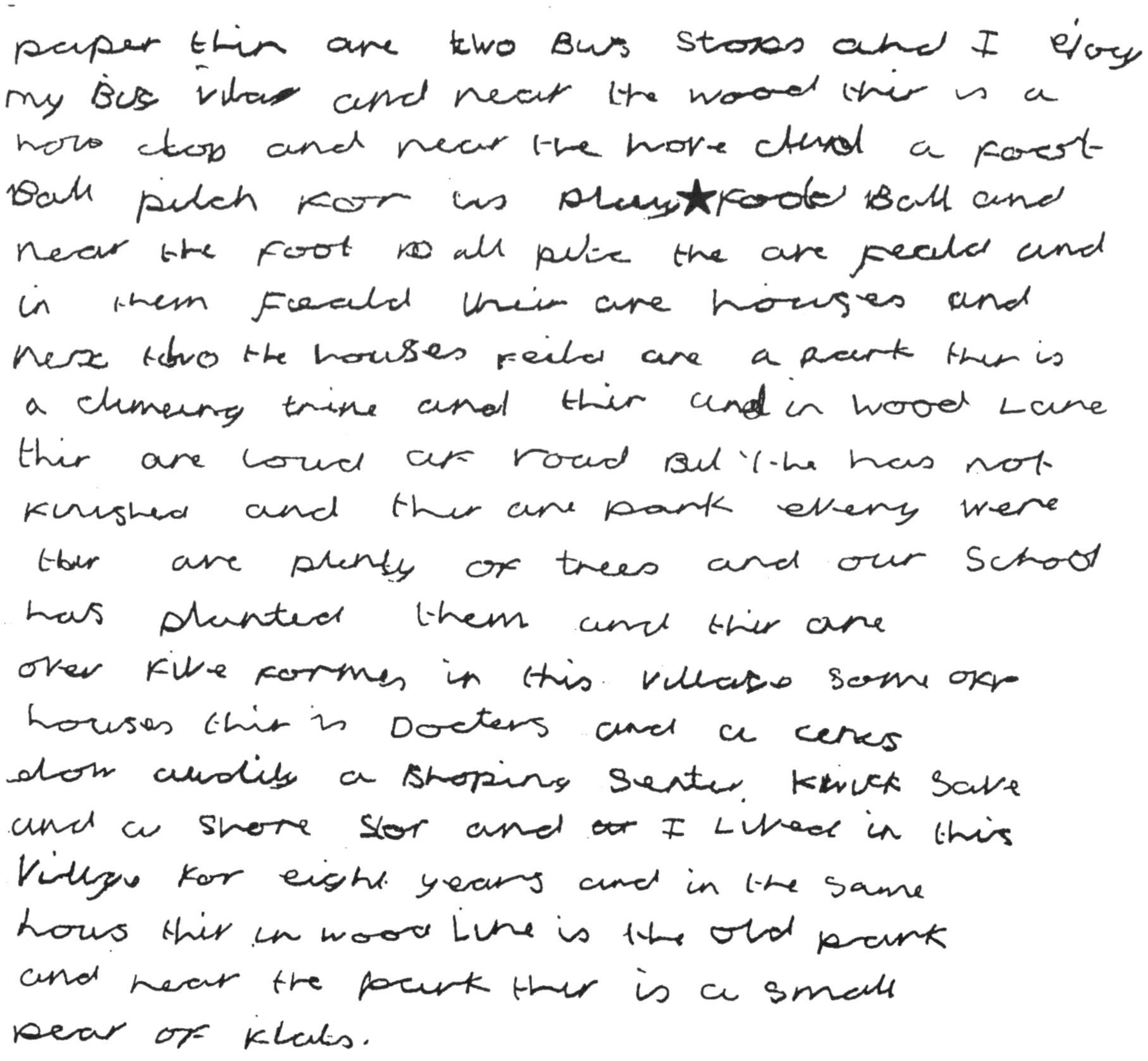
paper thin are two Bus Stops and I e/oy
my Bus ridas and near the wood thir is a
hore chop and near the hore church a foot-
Ball pitch for us play★foote Ball and
near the foot ro all pike the are feald and
in them feald their are houses and
nese two the houses feild are a park thir is
a climeing trine and thir and in wood Lane
thir are loud ar road but the has not
kinished and thir are park every were
thir are plenty of trees and our School
has planted them and thir are
over five formes in this village some of
houses thir is Docters and a ceres
dow audity a Shoping Senter, Kwik Save
and a Shore Stor and ar I Lived in this
Villge for eight years and in the same
hous thir in wood Line is the old park
and near the park thir is a small
pear of klats.

Figure 21 - A sample of written work from a right handed boy, aged 10 years 5 months.

Guidance for the assessment of Figure 21 for grammatical features

On the positive side:

- the boy writes at length and has much to write about;
- the asterisk indicates that he wrote 296 words in the 20 minute period, placing him in the ranks of the fastest writers in Year 6.

Problems occur with:

- his writing of the following word strings:

'were thir are'

'not much shops'

'thir is now mane road'

'their is not much cars'

Teaching objectives in the order of priority might be:

- use one of the writer's own scripts to show how the writing can be broken into sentences;
- use a pencil mark surround to delineate sentences in his own writing:

  'our village is a place were thir are menny krickent clubs'

  'one a dog stok in this Big hole';
- use strips of paper on which complete sentences can be written;
- teach the difference between the use of 'much' and 'many',

  e.g. if one can count the items, then the word 'many' is used.

  'Much' is used to refer to a continuous commodity.

CHAPTER 13

Logical, Stylistic and Expressive Features of Writing

National Curriculum requirements

Key Stage One Programme of Study states that pupils should:

- be taught to write independently on subjects that are of interest and importance to them;
- organise and present their writing in different ways, for different tasks and for different readers;
- be taught to write in the narrative forms of stories and diaries, to compose poems, and to write notes which include lists and captions. They should be able to record observations and write messages in the forms of notices, information and instructions;
- be able to make choices about vocabulary and to organise imaginative and factual writing in different ways.

Pupils should be able to discuss the organisation of their writing and the way in which sentences link together. Their interest in words and their meaning should be developed to include words with similar meanings, opposites, and words with more than one meaning.

Key Stage Two Programme of Study states that pupils should:

- be taught how to use paragraphs, linking sentences together coherently;
- learn how to use writing as a means of developing, organising and communicating ideas;
- be encouraged to develop the ability to write in forms characteristic of argument, commentary, narrative and dialogue;
- know how to distinguish degrees of formality in writing suitable for unfamiliar audiences, as appropriate to writing guide books, pamphlets and reviews.

In general, pupils should be able to identify their audience and purpose, making careful choices of vocabulary, and constructing effective, well organised sentences and paragraphs in order to make meaning clear and interesting to a reader.

Putting some of the recommendations into practice, the writer might, for example: be able to write a story for younger children; report on a visit, and advise on its suitability for other groups; inform a new member of the school about what will be expected of him or her, or about what the school curriculum has to offer. If this were well done, I am sure that potential pupils' parents would be interested to hear the views of established pupils. However, virtually all narrative will be written with an audience or reader in mind, and this should be borne in mind during the writing task. At a formal level, where structure of writing is emphasised, the features of these kinds of writing might be:

- using an opening paragraph;
- writing a sequence of real or imagined events coherently in chronological accounts;
- writing stories which have an opening, setting, characters, series of events and solution;
- writing instructions for the completion of a particular task;
- writing a detailed account of an experiment in which sequence is crucial to success;
- using different written language, as appropriate, for different audiences, e.g. in a friendly or formal letter; in a personal memo or formal report;
- writing so that varying points of view are presented and discussed;
- writing a final paragraph on each occasion.

Character description, attitudes and emotions have a role in creative and imaginative writing. When writing is of this nature, expressive and perhaps including an exploratory exercise, pupils can be involved in the task from its inception. They can discuss the targeted audience, and what that audience might like to read or be involved in. They could discuss the proposed project with the audience before the writing is begun, and eventually discuss the success or otherwise of the outcome.

Gill Hackett (1989) followed this kind of procedure with a group of Year 5 and 6 pupils who had seemed to find little satisfaction in writing or in their completed writing tasks. The teacher's suggestion was that they should write stories for children in the infant classes and that, when completed, the stories might be presented in book form with pictures and the usual picture and print formats. The writers became engaged in the kinds of activities that most successful writers will have engaged in at some time in their writing lives, for example, looking at books similar to the proposed ones in a library, identifying the kinds of characters usually adopted by writers of books for children, the relative distribution of pictures and print, and so on. In Gill Hackett's exercise, discussion occurred between the younger children and the older writers. Stories were written, and an evaluation of successful and less successful aspects followed. This kind of exercise can be a real life simulation for pupils in school. It could occur for expressive and imaginative writing, or when teaching pupils to report incidents of a more factual nature.

Imaginative reader/audience monitoring exercises are likely to be fruitful and interesting for young writers. The fact that a targeted audience is identified gives a 'raison d'etre' for writing at all and for writing well when the task is undertaken. It is intended that the formalities of writing should serve the requirements of the purpose of writing. The two aspects: good standards in secretarial skills and presentation, and worthiness of the targeted audience, go hand in hand when writing flourishes in school.

Try assessing *Figure* 22 from a logical, stylistic and expressive point of view. Use the assessment/teaching model for your own attempt.

Our Village 19.6.92

The village that I live in is quite small, but I would rather have it ~~smaller~~ small because you can find your way around the village better. One of the main things that I like about Wood Lane is that it is very quite and there arnt much traffic about the roads, so then you can play on the roads and than the traffic is comming racing past all the time. I enjoy living in wood lane also because I have got alot of friends who live here, and when I am playing on my own and I get board then I will go and call for one of my friends. A could thing about Woodlane is that he has a Youth club and attached on to the Youth club is a little park and also there is a football pich where anybody can play football or ride your bike on there. next to the youth club on one side is the woods, and that is where I go for walks or somthing, and on the other side of the Youth club is a club, I somtimes go to the club with my dad. In Church street there is a post office and that is a very good shop, but it's only little and you can hardly get around the shop.

In Wood lane there use to be a buchers shop but now it has been closed down. There is quite alot of vandalism in wood lane, there is alot of vandalism down the youth club and by the bus shelter★ If I Could make somchanges in Wood Lane I would start by putting Wood Lane Chapel in Dudley and

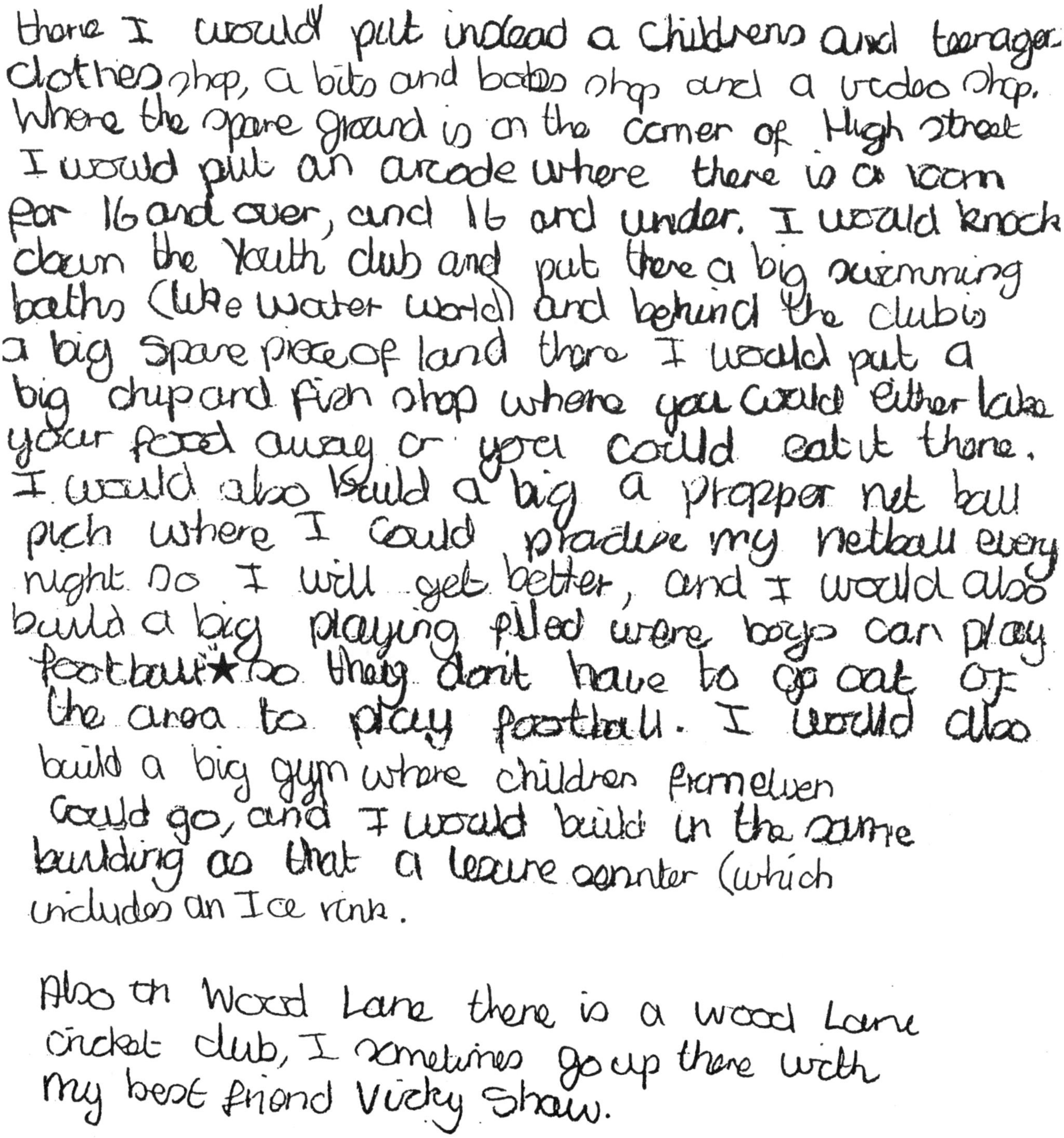

there I would put indead a childrens and teenager clothes shop, a bits and bobs shop and a video shop. Where the spare ground is on the corner of High street I would put an arcade where there is a room for 16 and over, and 16 and under. I would knock down the Youth club and put there a big swimming baths (like water world) and behind the club is a big spare piece of land there I would put a big chip and fish shop where you could either take your food away or you could eat it there. I would also build a big a propper net ball pich where I could practise my netball every night so I will get better, and I would also build a big playing filed were boys can play football★ so they don't have to go out of the area to play football. I would also build a big gym where children from eleven could go, and I would build in the same building as that a leaure center (which includes an Ice rink.

Also in Wood Lane there is a wood Lane cricket club, I sometimes go up there with my best friend Vicky Shaw.

Figure 22 - A sample of writing from a right-handed girl, aged 11 years 5 months.

An assessment of the sample of writing in Figure 22

On the positive side:

- the writer writes at length and is able to give much information about the village of Wood Lane. Her description gives an excellent impression of the village for the reader. The script also reflects the fact that the writer is reaching the age when she will look further afield for things to do, but would rather like facilities close at hand in her own village, for the time being;

- she writes 167 words in the 20 minute period, placing her in the upper average speed/output range for pupils in her year group;

- she writes good sentences with appropriate punctuation.

Problems occur in:

- the lack of any evidence of planning;

- lack of recognition that the changes to the village which she advocates would destroy aspects, such as small size and quietness, that she initially describes as advantages.

Teaching objectives in order of priority might be:

- suggest that she should begin with a simple description of Wood Lane;

- next, she might write about the advantages of living in Wood Lane;

- disadvantages of living in Wood Lane might follow this;

- finally, she could suggest changes, with some recognition of what the implications of change might be;

- paragraphing follows logically from planning and dividing up the script;

  (This kind of writing exercise can, of course, be written in either of two writing genres. It can be intended as a factual and informative report for someone who has little information about the subject matter, or it can be a story type exercise, perhaps a letter to a distant friend, describing the writer's feeling about the village at the present time.)

- the purpose of writing inevitably influences written style, and this can be pointed out to Year 5 and 6 pupils.

CHAPTER 14

Examining Writing at Wood Lane County Primary School

Writing is such an everyday school task that it may often be pursued with little thought about what occurs when children write. What kinds of demand does writing put on children? Do they vary their approaches when tackling different kinds of writing and, perhaps most important, does their writing improve as they progress through school? Does practice make perfect, or do they go on practising weaknesses, so that little progress can be seen from one school year to the next? Chapter 3 has shown that it is possible for some children to make little progress in writing, despite the considerable number of school hours that it occupies.

Teachers at Wood Lane County Primary School were interested in pupils' writing long before this exercise began. However, they regarded a request that they should participate in a special writing project with enthusiasm. This would provide them with an opportunity to look more closely at the writing process, and would give the pupils a motivating activity for the last weeks of the 1992/93 school year. They chose titles from different sections of the lists offered (Chapter 6), so that children in different year groups completed writing with a range of titles.

Writing by pupils in Years 3, 4 and 5

Year 3 pupils were given three titles, with no preparatory discussion:

> 'Water', with the instruction, 'Imagine someone has never seen a swimming pool or the sea. Describe the water and how they could learn to swim';
>
> My favourite person;
>
> A newspaper report.

Preparatory discussion took place between teacher and pupils before the next titles were attempted:

> Our village;
>
> A visit to a supermarket;
>
> A letter inviting parents to an end of year open afternoon.

All Year 4 and the younger Year 5 pupils were given the following titles with no preparatory discussion:

> My favourite person;
>
> Water - 'Imagine someone had never seen a swimming pool or the sea. Describe the water and how they could learn to swim';
>
> A newspaper report.

Preparatory discussion took place between teacher and pupils before the next titles were attempted:

> Our village;
>
> A visit to the supermarket;
>
> A letter to the newspaper about how the village could be improved.

All Year 6 pupils and older Year 5 pupils were given the following titles with no preparatory discussion:

> My favourite person;
>
> A visit to the supermarket.

Preparatory discussion of varying degrees took place between teacher and pupils before the next titles were attempted:

> Our village;
>
> A letter to parents to inform them about an end of term event;
>
> A newspaper report;
>
> Imagine someone has never seen a swimming pool or the sea. Describe water and how they could learn to swim.

For all writing, children were instructed to place an asterisk after 20 minutes of writing, so that comparison of writing speeds and output could be made when necessary.

It is clearly not possible to analyse all of the pupils' writing, therefore only a small selection of examples has been included. Even in Year 3, at the age of eight years, writing performance varied considerably. Among the better writers, two children wrote 166 and 99 words in 20 minutes respectively, placing them at the top end of writing speed norms. Between them, they were able to spell 'would', 'being', 'pulled', 'floor', 'absolutely', 'creatures', 'describe', and 'millions', correctly. Since our concern is principally with special needs, *Figures* 23, 24 and 25 are worthy of more detailed consideration.

General observations concerning the three scripts

All the children write with very upright or variable slant. This is indicative of the fact that, initially, they had been taught print script for two or three years, and began to join letters early in the following school year. They have retained the very upright model. The following procedures will help:

- Check the posture of all children:
  - Do they sit comfortably?
  - Are tables and chairs of suitable height?

- Check forearm position in relation to paper:
    - The writing forearm should always be more or less parallel to the edge of the writing paper.
- Instruct left and right-handers about paper position:
    - The right hander should tilt the top of the paper towards the left.
    - The left hander should tilt the top of the paper towards the right.
- Suggest to the children that they might find it more comfortable to slope their writing slightly towards the right.

The major needs of each child, and the priorities for teaching objectives will now be dealt with individually.

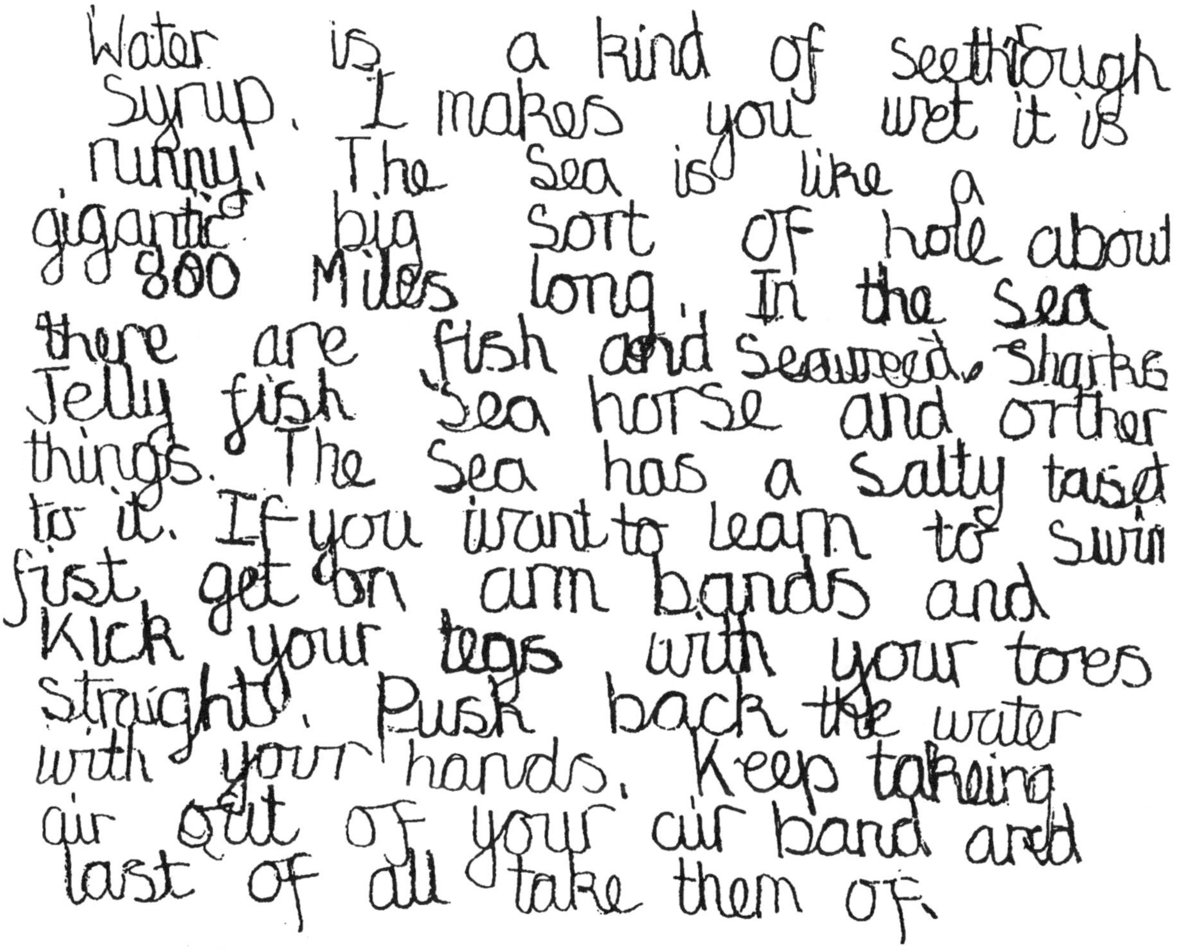

Water is a kind of seethrough syrup. I makes you wet it is runny. The Sea is like a gigantic big sort of hole about 800 Miles long. In the sea there are fish and seaweed. Sharks Jelly fish Sea horse and orther things. The Sea has a salty tasd to it. If you want to learn to swin fist get on arm bands and kick your legs with your toes straight. Push back the water with your hands. Keep takeing air out of your air band and last of all take them of.

Figure 23 - Sample of writing from a right-handed, Year 3 girl, aged 8 years.

Figure 23

This writing was completed by a right-handed girl who was exactly eight years of age. She wrote 58 words in 20 minutes, which is a little below average for her age group. However, she wrote carefully, with reasonably accurate spelling, and her large writing took her longer than if she had used a smaller, running (slightly slanted) script. On the positive side:

- she has a good 'turn of phrase', when she writes 'Water is a kind of see through syrup';
- she has taken care with both writing and spelling;
- writing in sentences is well understood and utilised.

Teaching objectives might be:

- observe posture and paper position so that weaknesses can be corrected;
- suggest that diagonal letter joins would make some letters more legible and increase writing speed. For example, in this writing, most letters which should have diagonal joins, are joined along the baseline;
- although spelling is good, occasional words can be identified for teaching. 'Other' is a commonly used word and is spelt 'orther', 'taste' is spelt here as 'taset'. It can be used to teach 'taste, haste, paste' etc. 'Takeing' shows that the rule for dropping 'e' before 'ing' is not known.

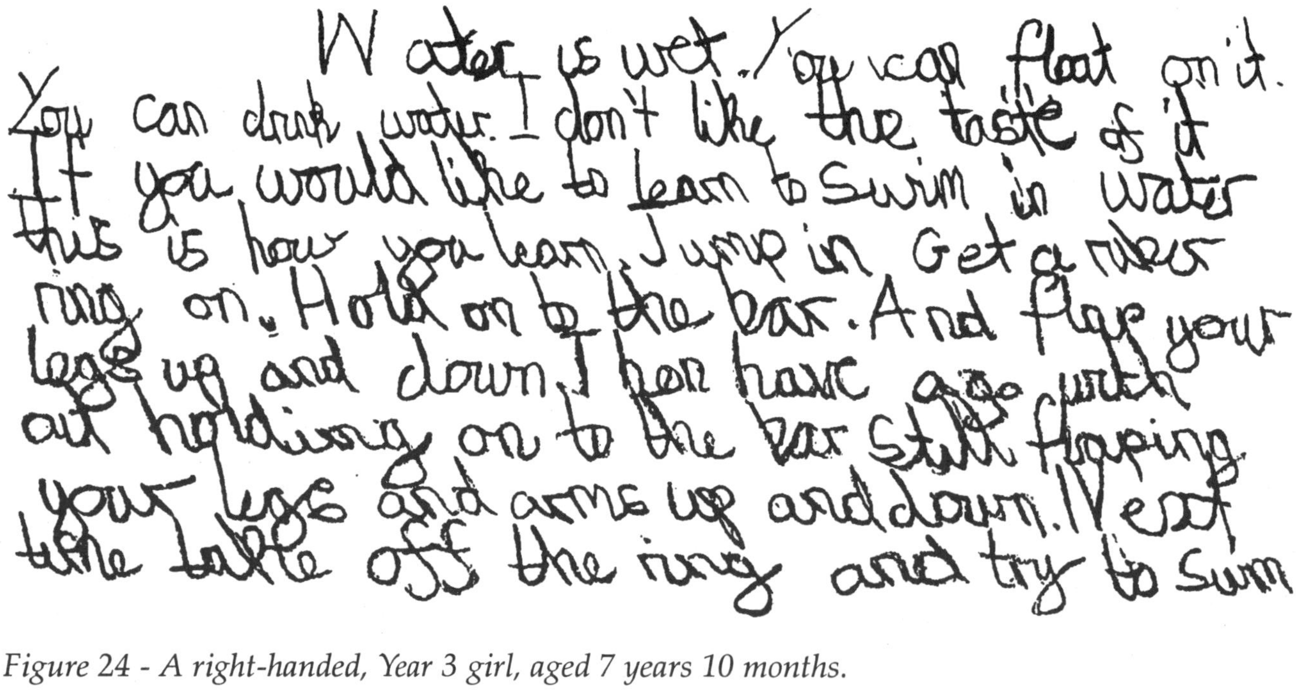

Figure 24 - A right-handed, Year 3 girl, aged 7 years 10 months.

Figure 24

This right-handed girl, aged seven years ten months, writes in short correct sentences, and has reasonably good spelling. She joins all letters within words, and seems to be held up a little by her joined writing efforts. On the positive side:

- she is writing slowly and carefully;
- there are only two spelling errors;
- she is able to write instructions in sequence.

Teaching objectives might be:

- keep the writing paper at a similar angle, i.e. with the side parallel to the writing forearm, so that the slant will be consistent;
- tilt the top of the paper to the left;
- space out words to make the writing easier to read;
- writing which is slightly sloped towards the right would increase writing speed and make the writer more comfortable;
- diagonal rather than horizontal joins from the appropriate letters (egs. 'a', 'e', 'c', 'd') will help to increase speed and make the writing more legible;
- show how the consonants 'b' in rubber, and 'p' in flapping should be doubled after the short vowels 'u' and 'a';
- use the opportunity to talk about sequence, i.e. it would be sensible to put on the rubber ring before jumping into the water.

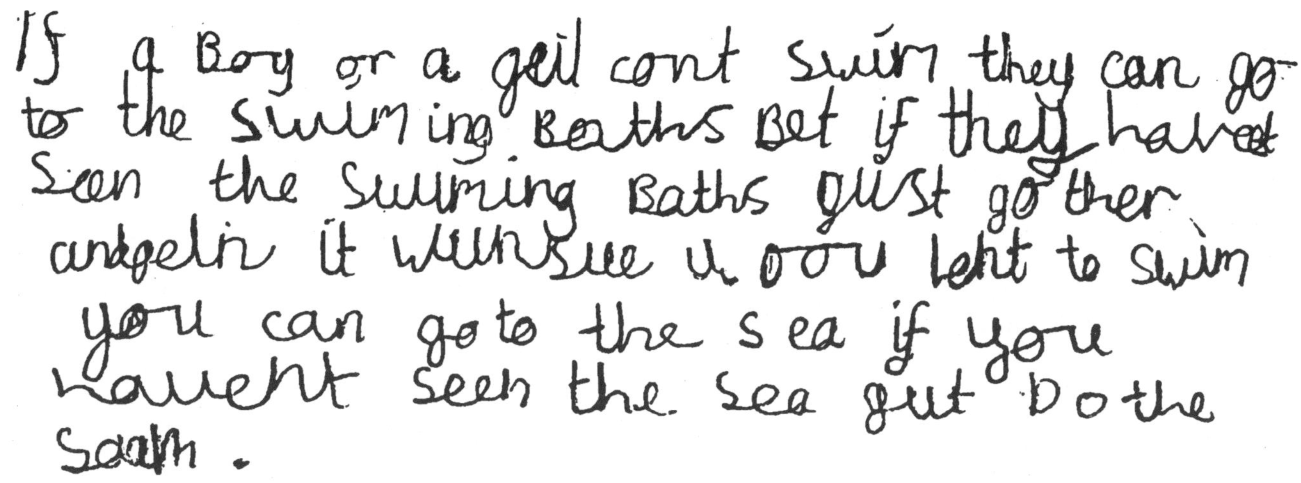

Figure 25 - A left-handed, Year 3 boy, aged 8 years 9 months.

Figure 25
This left-handed boy is one of the older members of his class. He wrote 48 words in 20 minutes which places him in the lower, though not the lowest, writing-speed range. He makes good attempts at spelling, and writes in a logical sequence. On the positive side:

- he makes a good attempt at writing and spelling;
- many letters are formed in the correct direction, to aid joined writing;
- he writes a number of Key Words correctly, for example:

  'if', 'a', 'boy', 'or', 'a', 'swim', 'they', 'can', 'go', 'to', 'the', 'baths', 'seen', 'and', 'you', 'sea'.

Teaching objectives might be:

- check that his posture and paper position are comfortable, and suitable for a left-handed writer;
- practise the common words that he already knows, checking that he writes comfortably and without postural stress;
- show that the pencil can be rested in some long words, so that writing is not dominated by excessive concern with joined writing;
- teach 'and get in', using the three separate words to illustrate letter joins in short words and spaces between the words;
- use 'and get in', to show how joins between some letters are diagonal rather than horizontal ones from one letter to the next. Use letter joins 'in' and '-im' as in 'swim' for this purpose.

With all three children, give *encouragement* first.

Writing by Year 6 and Older Year 5 pupils

For this class, the writing about 'Our Village' and the letter to parents were examined. The letter was to invite parents to an evening at school, entitled 'Round Up 92'. Although the children were to be present at the event and many were to participate and perhaps receive prizes, the task was difficult because of the large amount of information that needed to be transmitted to parents. The timing, the fact that refreshments would be served, that attendance was restricted to two adults per pupil, and that some younger children would be coming to help with refreshments, made the task a true test of being able to give only the essential information and to present it logically. A 'draft' and 'fair copy' were completed by all children.

Discussion of Figure 26 a and b

The writing of a right-handed boy, aged 10 years 5 months, is illustrated in *Figures 26 a and b. Figure a* shows his draft copy, and *Figure b* shows the redraft. Writing is clearly an arduous task for this boy, as shown by the asterisk in *Figure b.* The asterisk was written when 20 minutes had elapsed during the redrafting exercise, showing that he wrote 29 words or numerals in that period of time. Writing speeds can be checked with writing speed norms as shown in Chapter 15. The draft copy shows that the boy is able to write at length and probably feels a full participant in the school and its activities. He writes logically and gives all the essential information, for example, although the event begins at 7.30pm, it is important for the audience to be in their seats by 7.15pm. On the positive side:

- the boy writes at length and is able to transmit the message accurately;
- he writes in short manageable sentences;
- he forms letters in the correct direction;
- he knows quite a lot about letter joins.

Teaching objectives might be:

- he will use a capital letter to begin every sentence. He already knows the rule and omits the capital only occasionally;
- check his writing posture, pencil/pen, and pencil/pen hold. Ensure that each is appropriate and comfortable;
- ensure the paper slopes to the left, as for right handers;
- encourage a slight, consistent slope to the right, for writing;
- teach correct spelling for the commonly used words:

  'written' - Rule: The consonant is doubled after the short vowel';

  'please' - Rule: The vowel digraph 'ea occurs in 'please' 'weak' 'beak' 'leak' 'speak';

  'sincerely' - The syllable 'cere' requires the 'e' at the end;

- teach him *how* to learn by using the spelling method that works best for him.

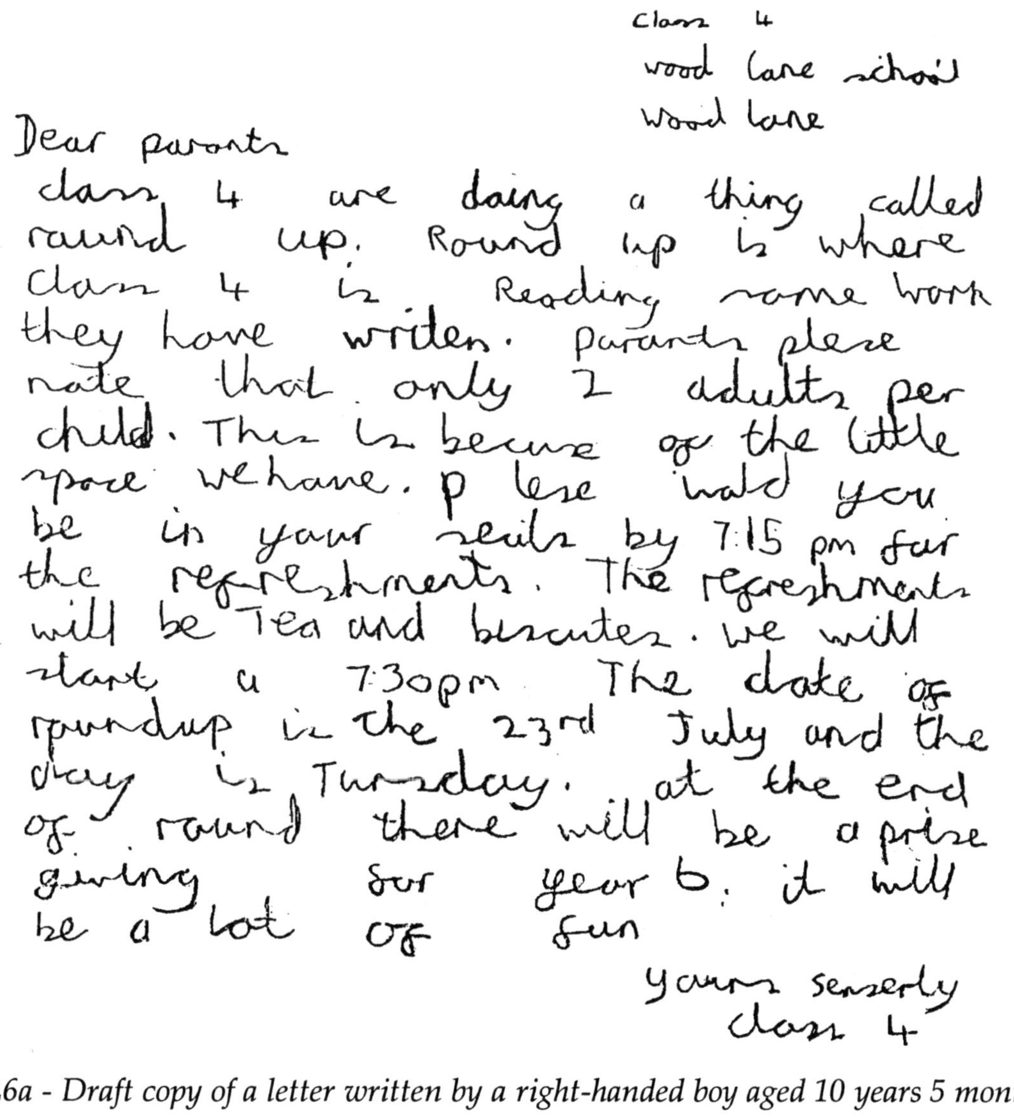

Class 4
wood lane school
Wood lane

Dear parents
class 4 are doing a thing called round up. Round up is where class 4 is Reading some work they have writen. parents plese note that only 2 adults per child. This is becuse of the little space we have. p lese would you be in your seats by 7:15 pm for the refreshments. The refreshments will be Tea and biscuites. we will start a 7:30pm The date of roundup is the 23rd July and the day is Tuesday. at the end of round there will be a prise giving for year 6. it will be a lot of fun

yours senserly
class 4

Figure 26a - Draft copy of a letter written by a right-handed boy aged 10 years 5 months.

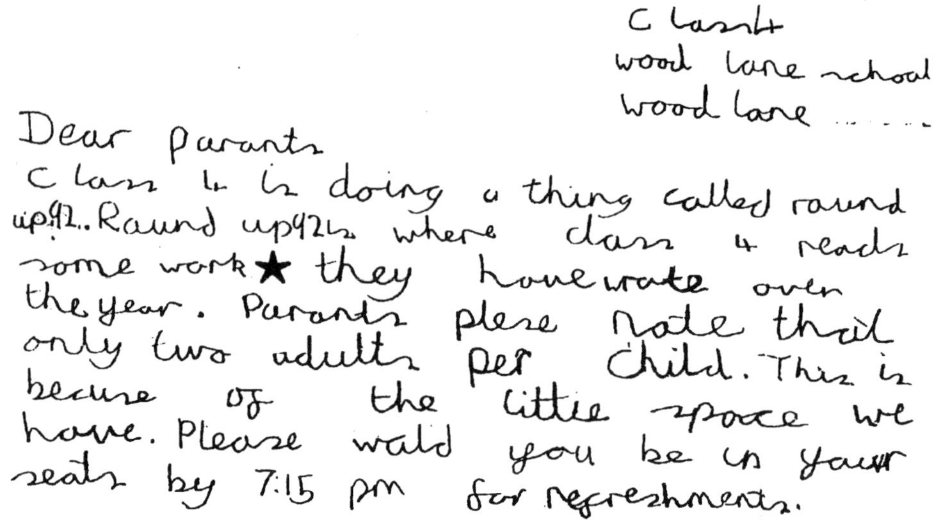

Class 4
wood lane school
wood lane

Dear parants
Class 4 is doing a thing called raund up92. Raund up92's where class 4 reads some work★ they have wrote over the year. Parants plese note that only two adults per child. This is becuse of the little space we have. Please wald you be in your seats by 7:15 pm for refreshments.

Figure 26b - Good copy (second draft) of the same letter.

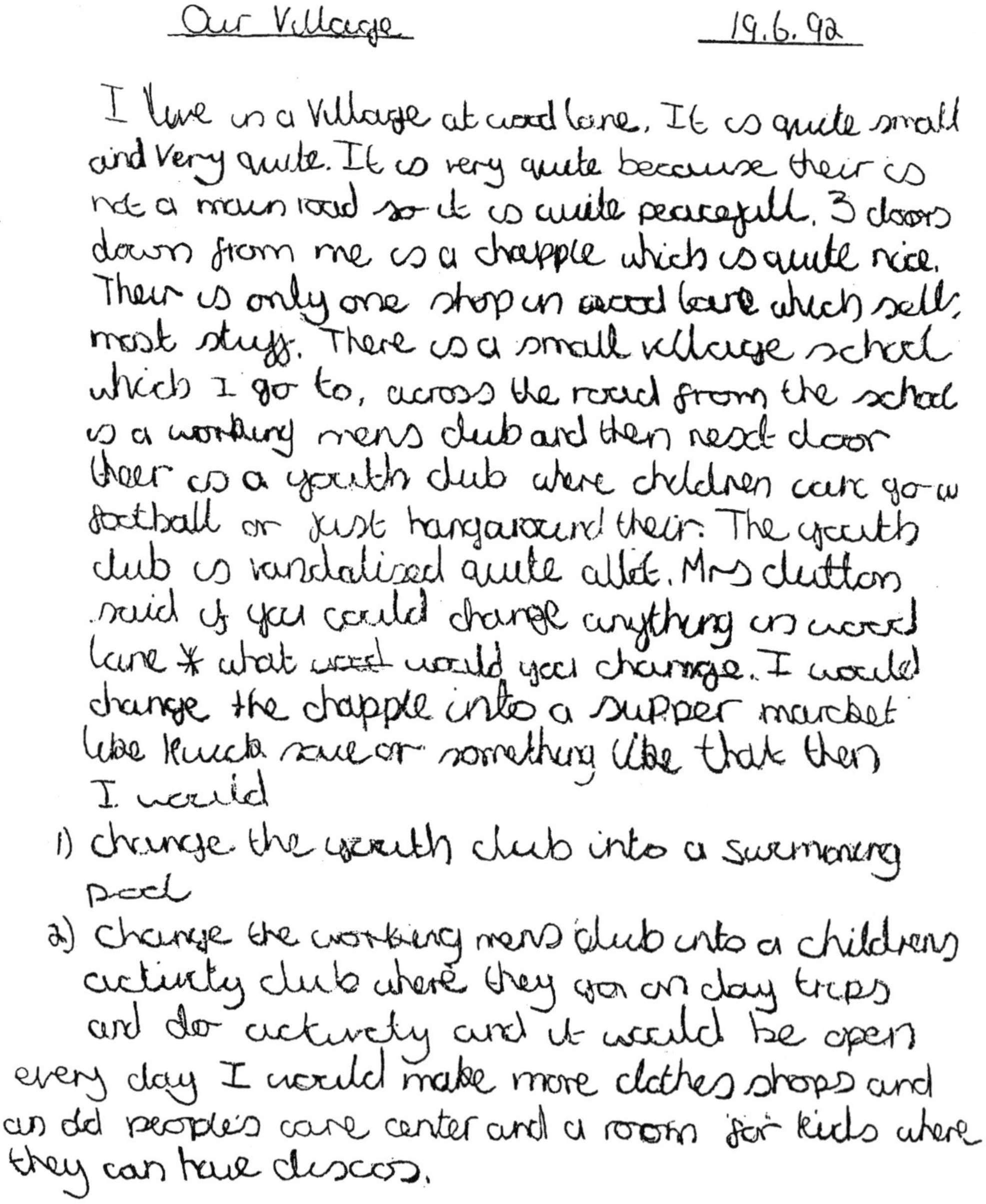

Our Village 19.6.92

I live in a Village at wood lane. It is quite small and Very quite. It is very quite because their is not a main road so it is quite peacefull. 3 doors down from me is a chapple which is quite nice. Their is only one shop in wood lane which sell's most stuff. There is a small village school which I go to, across the road from the school is a working mens club and then next door their is a youth club where children can go to football or just hangaround their. The youth club is vandalised quite allot. Mrs clutton said if you could change anything in wood lane ✱ what would you change. I would change the chapple into a supper market like kwick save or something like that then I would

1) change the youth club into a swimming pool
2) change the working mens club into a childrens activity club where they go on day trips and do activity and it would be open every day I would make more clothes shops and an old people's care center and a room for kids where they can have discos.

Figure 27 - A left-handed girl, aged 10 years 11 months, writes about the village where she lives.

Discussions of Figure 27

This was written by a more able girl who chose to write about the village of Wood Lane, where she lives. It is included here to give the reader an impression of the village, also to show how a more able ten-year-old manages the task. The piece is interesting and gives much information. One particular aspect is that, although she likes Wood Lane and is pleased to live there, she would change it in ways that could bring the convenient though often less desirable intrusions such as a supermarket and a disco. She writes 117 words in 20 minutes, as denoted by the asterisk. This places her in the lower average speed range for her age group.

On the positive side:

- she shows that she has ideas and is not short of things to write about;
- she is an average speller, who spells most commonly-used words accurately;
- her writing is usually, though not always, legible.

Teaching objectives might be:

- check writing posture and paper position to ensure the correct posture for left-handed writers;
- indicate how slight increase in word spacing could improve her legibility;
- ensure that letters are correctly formed so that 'm' does not lose a downstroke as in 'main' and 'mens', and 'w' does not lose an element as it does in 'Kuick save';
- teach spelling of commonly-used words:

  'quiet', 'there/their', 'a lot';

  'peaceful', 'plentiful', 'beautiful' - all have one 'l';
  'super' and similar words 'music', 'tunic', 'cubic' begin with open syllables 'su', 'mu', 'tu', 'cu', so the vowel says its proper name;

- show how she could set out her work in paragraphs. For example, in this piece of writing she could inform the reader about Wood Lane, where it is, how big, and so on.

Observations: Continuing policies and strategies

A reappraisal

The complete writing project was seen as an opportunity to reassess general school policy on encouraging pupils to write. Because the project was seen as a special series of writing tasks, teachers and pupils were able to view these tasks and outcomes with little reference to what normally occurred during writing periods in school. Both teachers and pupils inevitably had established perceptions of and expectations about what writing in school should be, and the project provided an opportunity to question them. Over the years, objectivity is inevitably eroded, and the opportunity to view externally requested assignments and tasks, and pupils responses to them, provided a useful fresh start to discussion about how constructive and enjoyable free writing periods could be planned.

Teachers are likely to differ in their choice of subjects for free written work and to have their own ideas about how pupils can best be encouraged to fulfil teacher expectations. They inevitably differ in the degree to which they 'prepare' pupils for the task, some giving few ideas of how tasks should be approached and some giving, perhaps, very prescribed outlines of what pupils should write about. Pupils, of course, receive teachers' suggestions from their own viewpoint. That the two viewpoints should be discussed may rarely occur to either pupils or teachers. Pupils begin very early to establish their individual perceptions of what teachers expect, and each teacher is likely to have added a little, and sometimes changed, what each pupil's perception becomes.

The outcomes of observations and discussions were as follows:

Teachers tended to believe -

- that all pupils like to have discussion about what is expected from a particular writing task;
- that all pupils benefit from preparatory discussion when it occurs;
- that able writers will inevitably have more of their own ideas and need less preparation;
- that less able writers would have little to write if teachers did not make several suggestions during the preparation period.

All teachers recognised that there would be pupils who did not exactly fit one of the well-defined categories of writer. However, there were a few useful conclusions which helped to shape changes for the future. For able pupils, there was to be a change of emphasis in the pre-writing discussion period. More able pupils, in particular, did not always wish to receive suggestions about the content of their work. They recognised that free written work was their opportunity to express individuality and originality, and that extra marks and recognition were sometimes awarded for this. If the teacher had already suggested what they themselves had intended to write, they could no longer regard it as their own contribution. However, the pupils who seemed to have little difficulty in writing extensively, did not always stop to plan their work and write constructively. They sometimes put pen to paper immediately and wrote in what was often an interesting though somewhat meandering style. This could be very acceptable within a section or paragraph of the writing, but was unlikely to be logical if pursued for a complete writing script. It would not help them to develop skills useful for the instructive and explanatory writing, that they would need in order to succeed in a range of subjects at top junior and secondary levels.

Writing problems begin early for less able writers. How writing skills can be extended is discussed at length in Chapter 2. However, if they write much less than their classmates from the beginning, the cumulative loss in terms of practice alone, is likely to become a major handicap. By the junior years, the habit of 'not knowing what to write' and of writing little, has usually become well established. These are the pupils who seem to benefit from teachers' suggestions and are relatively happy to adopt many of their ideas. The results are likely to be somewhat pedestrian and, above all, will give little satisfaction and sense of achievement for the writers. A special project, designed principally to convince them that they could write at length, was set up for this group of pupils.

Reluctant writers' project

Pupils in this project were principally those who struggled to get words on paper. Several had limited reading and spelling levels and were inevitably struggling to cope with basic secretarial skills. Their personal correctly written word bank remained in need of extension. Their writing content was suffering because of preoccupation with secretarial skills, and written output was limited in consequence. These pupils were at quite a different stage from their more able writing peers. They needed to reach the stage where words could flow from their pens. Their confidence was built as follows:

- They were given weekly sessions in groups of four.
- An interesting story, at appropriate readability level, and which could be read in 15 minutes or so, was selected.
- Each pupil had a copy of the story.
- The pupils read the story in turn, each reading just enough to generate interest and not so much that other pupils would become bored by listening to them.
- Long pauses were avoided by the teacher taking up the reading if necessary, though this was avoided by careful selection of the text.
- At the end of the reading aloud, each pupil scanned the story to remind him or her of its content.
- There was discussion about how reviews might be written, such as:

  Is is a good story?

  Are there aspects which are not so good?

  Who are the characters?

  Where does it take place?

  Could the story have been improved?

  For which age group might it be suitable?

- Each pupil wrote a review of the story for classmates who had not been involved.

Although the purpose was to convince reluctant writers that they could write at length, a degree of writing sequence was also built into the task. Pupils benefited in several ways. Because they were reading age-appropriate stories on a regular basis, their reading levels improved. They also benefited because their writing was now the focus of attention, which had not been possible in their class of 38 pupils. Emphasis was being placed on their special need, rather than the more general writing needs of their classmates. The benefit of this project can be seen in Robert's writing, each piece being written within 20 minutes. He benefited principally from knowing that he could retain information, and that he could write at length when the conditions were right for this to occur.

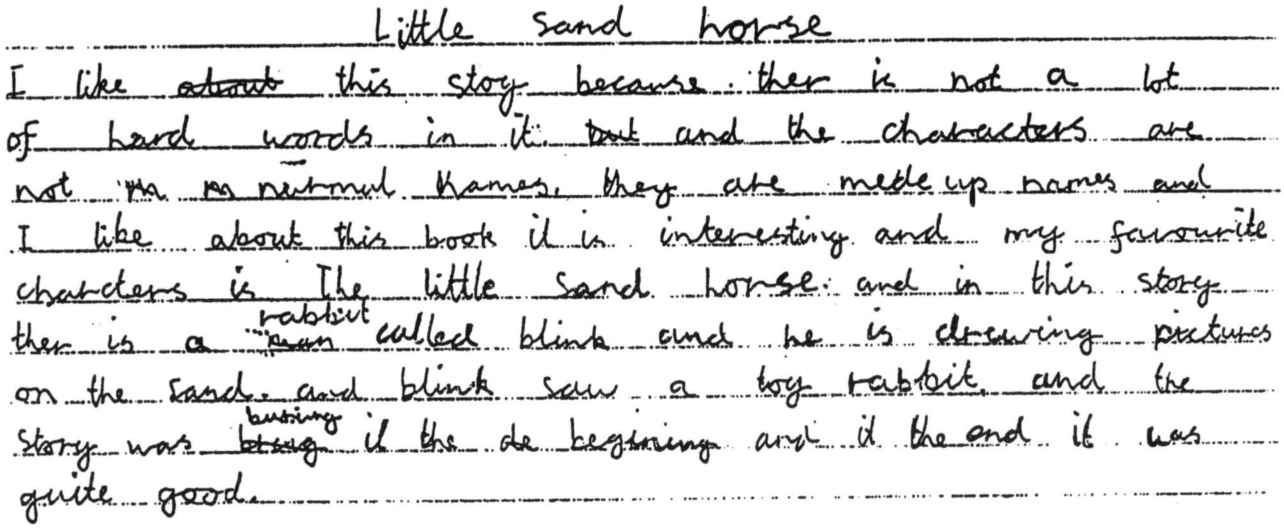

Little Sand horse

I like ~~about~~ this story because ther is not a lot of hard words in it ~~but~~ and the characters are not m m nutmul names they are metle up names and I like about this book it is interesting and my favourite charcters is The little Sand horse and in this story ther is a rabbit ~~man~~ called blink and he is drawing pictures on the sand and blink saw a toy rabbit and the story was boring ~~bing~~ it the de begining and it the end it was quite good.

Figure 28 - Robert's story review at the beginning of the reluctant writer project.

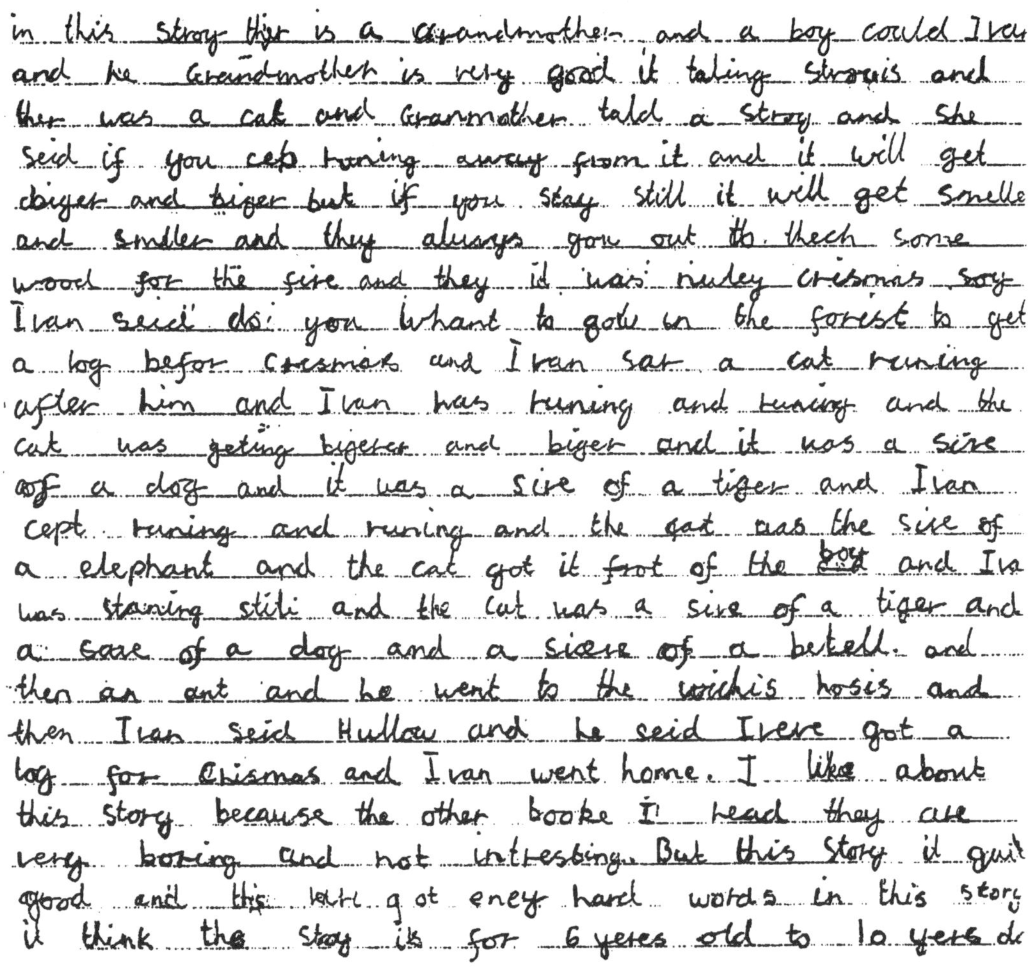

in this story ther is a Grandmother and a boy could Ivan and he Grandmother is very good it taling strois and ther was a cat and Granmother tald a story and she seid if you cep runing away from it and it will get biger and biger but if you stay still it will get smalle and smaller and they always gou out to fech some wood for the fire and they it was nirley crismas soy Ivan seid do you whant to gole in the forest to get a log befor Crismas and Ivan sat a cat runing after him and Ivan was runing and runing and the cat was geting bigeer and biger and it was a sire of a dog and it was a sire of a tiger and Ivan cept runing and runing and the cat was the sire of a elephant and the cat got it frot of the boy and Iva was staning stili and the cat was a sire of a tiger and a sare of a dog and a siere of a betell and then an ant and he went to the wichis hosis and then Ivan seid Hullow and he seid Ivere got a log for Crismas and Ivan went home. I like about this story because the other booke I head they are very boring and not intresting. But this story it quit good and this wark got eney hard words in this story i think the stay is for 6 yeres old to 10 yeres old

Figure 29 - Robert's story review after four reluctant writer project sessions.

A number of insights had emerged from the writing project as a whole. Some were related to teacher assumptions about how they should instruct or prepare pupils for free writing tasks. Others were about pupils' perceptions, the kinds of things they believed they were expected to write and, above all, how prescriptive the teachers' suggestions were intended to be.

Inevitably, the needs of eight-year-old writers are likely to be different from the needs of 11-year-old writers. The former are just getting going on writing, and the latter should be at the stage of writing logically, and introducing structure to their various kinds of written output.

Pupils who do not easily write well, and are potentially reluctant writers, need special consideration. Secretarial requirements need to be carefully delineated by each teacher and individual pupil's needs should be identified within the secretarial skill structure. As well as secretarial skills, there are those required for discursive writing. Pupils need to think about what they might write, retain individual thoughts in memory, and sequence them logically so that they will make sense to themselves as they re-read the script, and to any reader to whom the final script might be available. Ideally, the teacher's very difficult job is to identify the needs of every writer in both the secretarial and discursive areas of writing. This is clearly not possible within a large class of pupils, but it might be possible to identify groups of pupils who seem to have particular needs at any one time. In a class of ten-year-olds, for example, there will be those who still have little confidence to write and need to be shown how their written output can grow. There will be those whose major need is to strengthen spelling skills and who should be allowed to place their sole emphasis on spelling for a particular period of time. Some will have reached the confident writer stage much later than their peers and may then need considerable help with punctuation. The writer whose oral grammatical errors persist in written work may need a period of placing attention on grammatical skills, until some progress is made.

We currently hear much of the need for differentiation as a means of delivering the curriculum to all pupils. Writing probably makes the greatest demands on teachers, first because it is so complex, and second because its progress or otherwise influences achievement in so many curricular subjects.

Teachers at Wood Lane School were continuing to recognise the great demands that the teaching of writing entails. Participation in a general writing project, and experience of a specific project for eight reluctant writers, contributed to general understanding and led to the initiation of some change to the school's writing policy.

CHAPTER 15

A Standardised Writing Test

National Curriculum requirements are placing greater demands, not only on pupils' writing skills, but also on ability to write speedily and coherently under test or examination conditions. For example, from 1992, pupils no longer have been assessed totally or principally on coursework. The contribution of coursework marks are restricted, and examination marks have the greatest influence on 16+ final grades. Spelling, punctuation and grammar are awarded 5 per cent of all marks in both examinations and coursework at 16 + . Assessment at Key Stages 2 (11 +) and 3 (14+) lays some emphasis on written examinations. English, in particular, will require rigorous and sustained writing. Inevitably, 'how much' pupils manage to write as well as writing content and quality will have a bearing on pupils' achievement.

There is considerable evidence that the amount of writing produced by pupils in Year 3 is a valid indicator of both amount and quality of writing in the later junior school years (Alston, 1990). For this reason, teachers should be alerted to the needs of the underachieving writer as soon as the evidence becomes available. A standardised writing task at 8 + can provide an early screening measure from which pupils 'at risk' can be identified. Of course, standardised screening measures (tests) for reading, spelling, verbal and non-verbal reasoning, have been employed by some local education authorities for 25 years, or more. It seems probable that standardised written output could give a more valid prediction of what pupils will be able to achieve in school.

Norms for Cheshire pupils in Years 3 to 6 are presented in *Figures 30* to *37*. The graphs for each year group show measures of words and letters respectively. Table 1 gives further information about how much writing was obtained from pupils in the respective age groups.

A task similar to that completed by a representative sample of 500 Cheshire children could easily be reproduced in any school so that written output for that school could be monitored. The tasks on which the evidence was based and with which trials from any school might be compared, are as follows:

1. Pupils are given lined paper with the following measurements:

   length: 205 millimetres
   width: 180 millimetres
   line ruling: 8 millimetre intervals

2. Pupils are allowed to write with the usual writing tool (pen or pencil as appropriate).

3. They are instructed to write on one of the following topics: 'My favourite person (or Personality)'; 'Someone I know very well', or 'Something in which I am very interested'.

4. They are given brief encouraging instructions, such as, 'It can be about an animal, a friend, relative, television or sports personality; anyone you know a lot about, or something you know a lot about.'

5. The instructions continue, 'After 20 minutes, you will be asked to make a **cross** after the word you have just written'.

6. 'You can then go on writing until the end of the lesson'.

Teachers may not wish to count letters and/or words for most of their pupils. However, they may be particularly interested in those with greatest output, and certainly in those who write little. Some verbally able pupils may also draw attention to their plight if there are evident discrepancies between oral and written skills. The numbers of letters and/or words children write can be compared with the graphs to see how much children are able to write in the 20 minute period. Table 1 gives further information about age related written output.

	Letters		Words	
	Mean	**Range**	**Mean**	**Range**
Year 3	285	39 - 792	75	11- 215
Year 4	429	87 -1028	113	28 - 295
Year 5	451	126-1168	120	33 - 303
Year 6	585	221-1499	153	54 - 393

Table 1 - Means and ranges of letters and words written in a 20 minute period by Years 3, 4, 5 and 6 pupils.

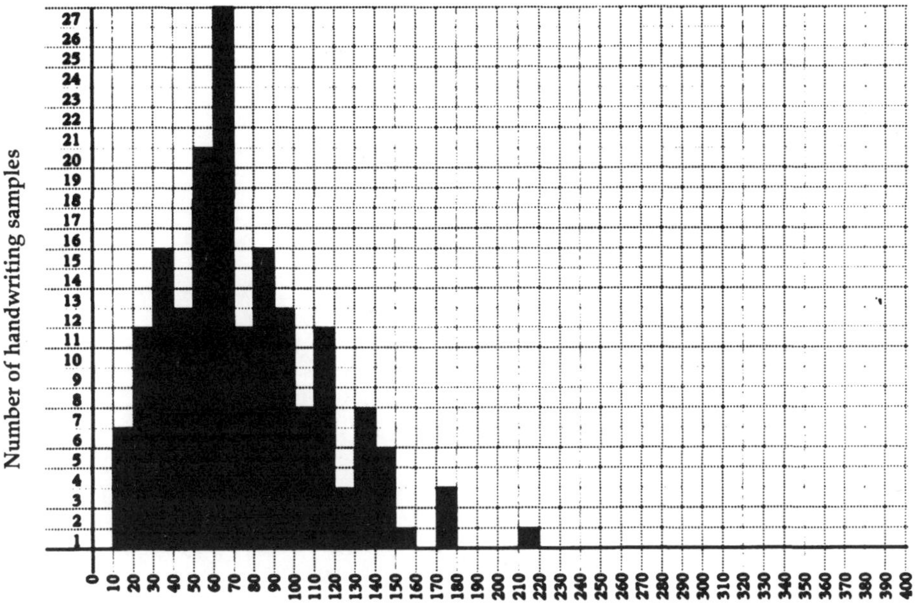

Figure 30 - Total number of words written in 20 minutes by Year 3 pupils.

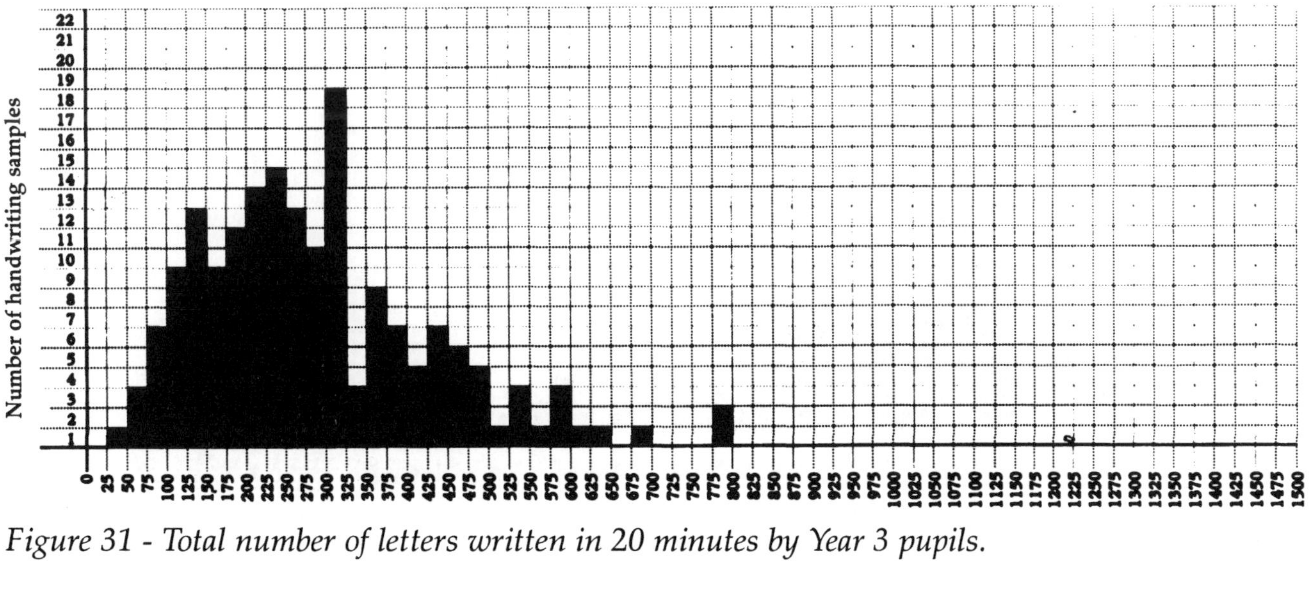

Figure 31 - Total number of letters written in 20 minutes by Year 3 pupils.

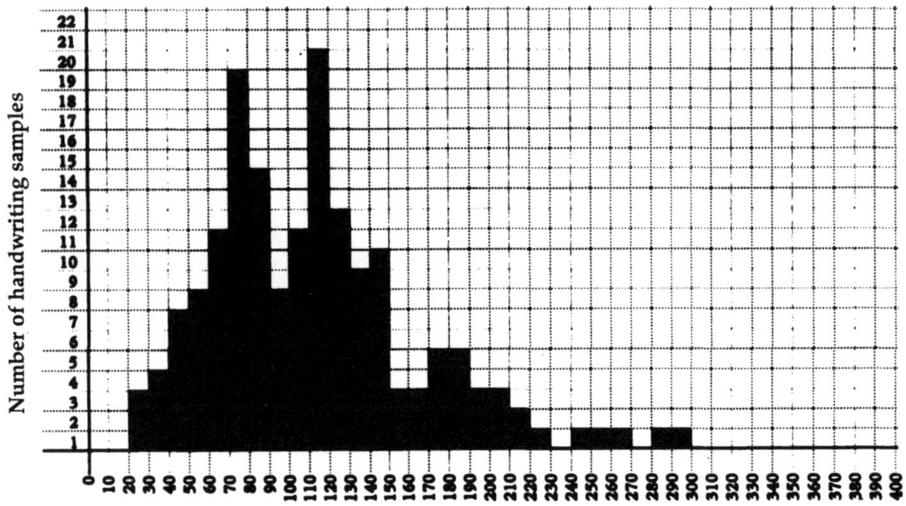

Figure 32 - Total number of words written in 20 minutes by Year 4 pupils.

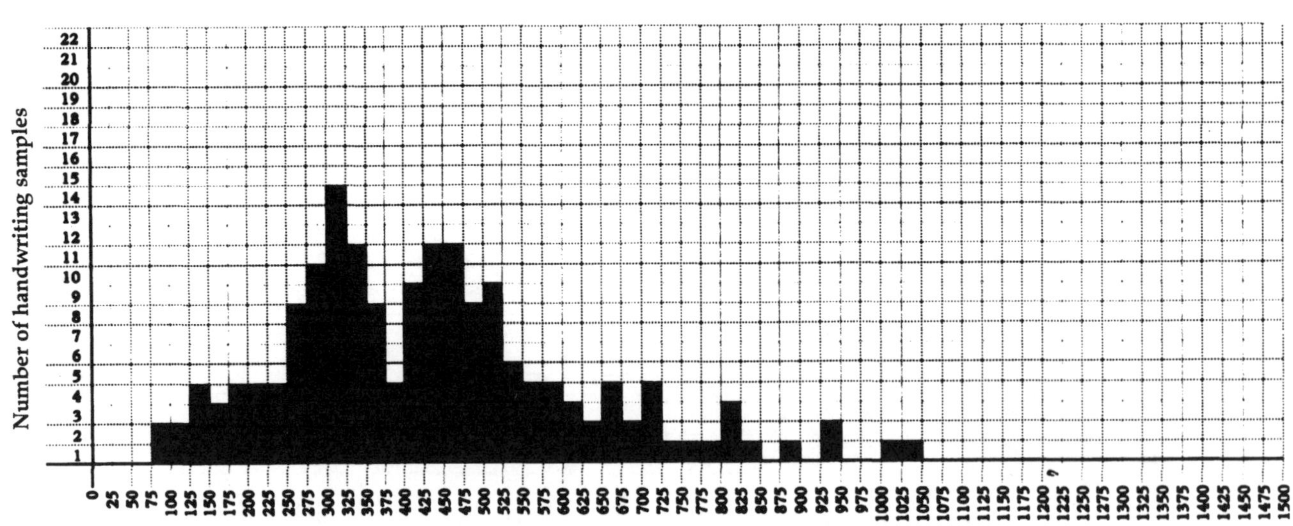

Figure 33 - Total number of letters written in 20 minutes by Year 4 pupils.

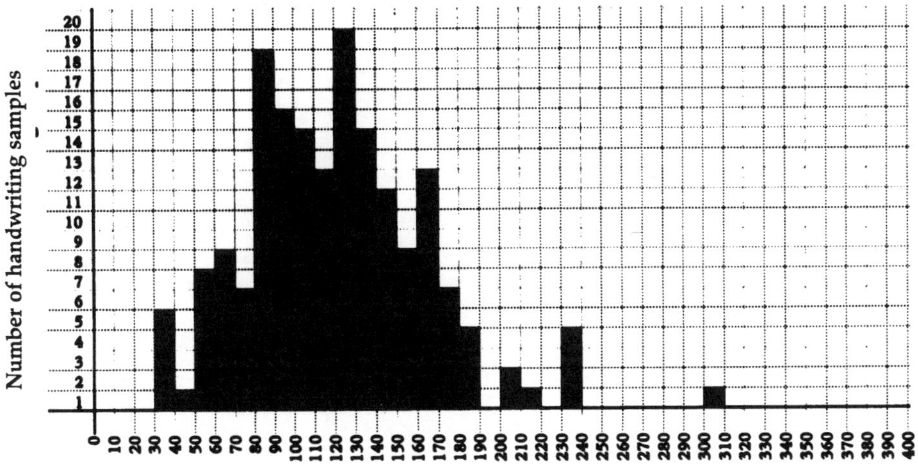

Figure 34 - Total number of words written in 20 minutes by Year 5 pupils.

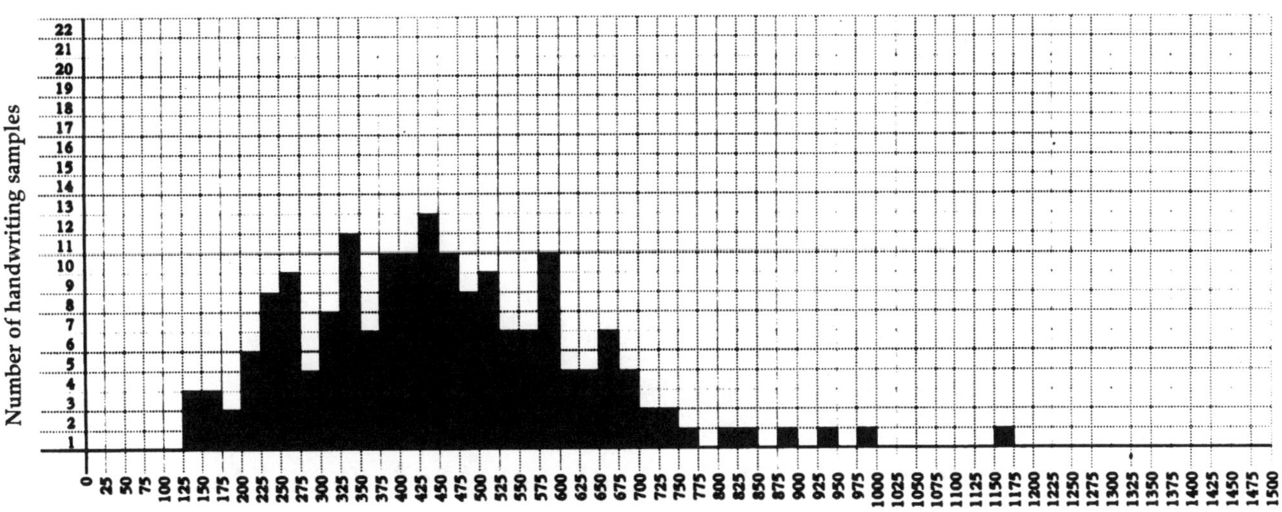

Figure 35 - Total number of letters written in 20 minutes by Year 5 pupils.

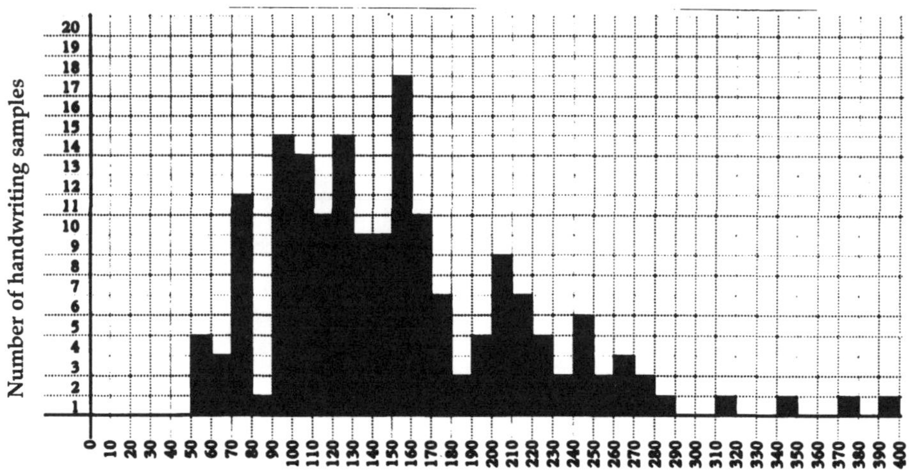

Figure 36 - Total number of words written in 20 minutes by Year 6 pupils.

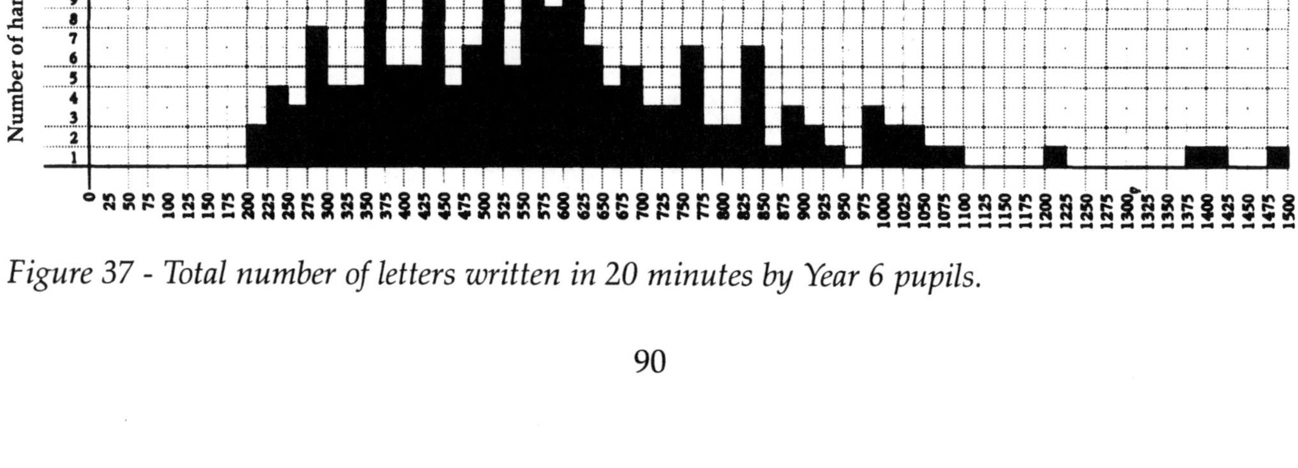

Figure 37 - Total number of letters written in 20 minutes by Year 6 pupils.

For years 3 to 6 on each writing occasion, total words written in the 20 minute period are counted. The total is divided by 20 to find words per minute, and each pupil's written output can be compared with that for the representative sample of Cheshire pupils.

The bars either side of the dotted line graphs, *Figures 39 and 40,* indicate scores which are one standard deviation from the average score. Sixteen per cent of pupils can be expected to score more than one standard deviation above the mean, and 16 per cent can be expected to score more than one standard deviation below the mean. The low and high scoring pupils are likely to be amongst the pupils deserving special attention from their teachers.

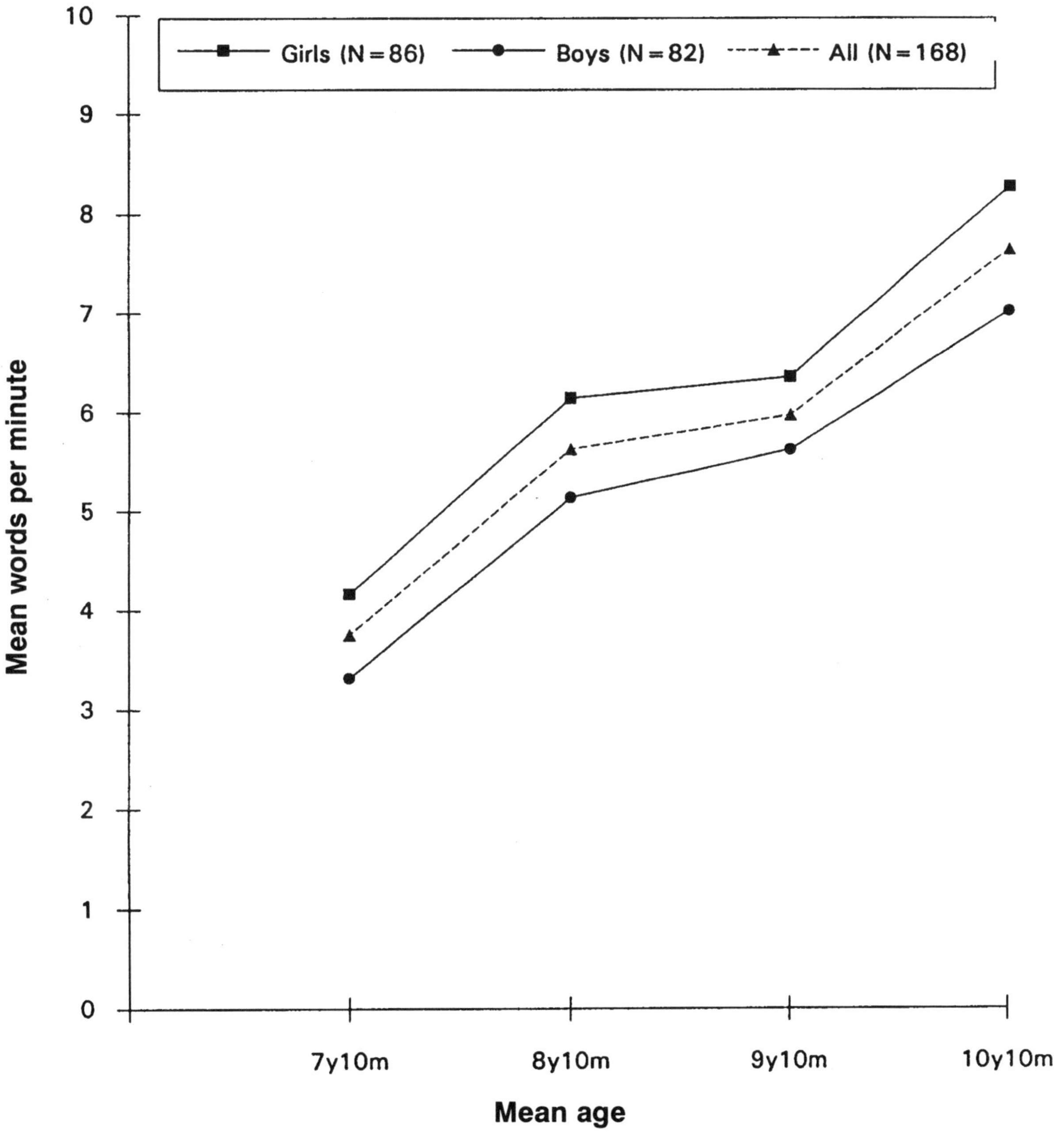

Figure 38 - Cheshire Primary School pupils (19 schools): Writing output over 20 minute period.

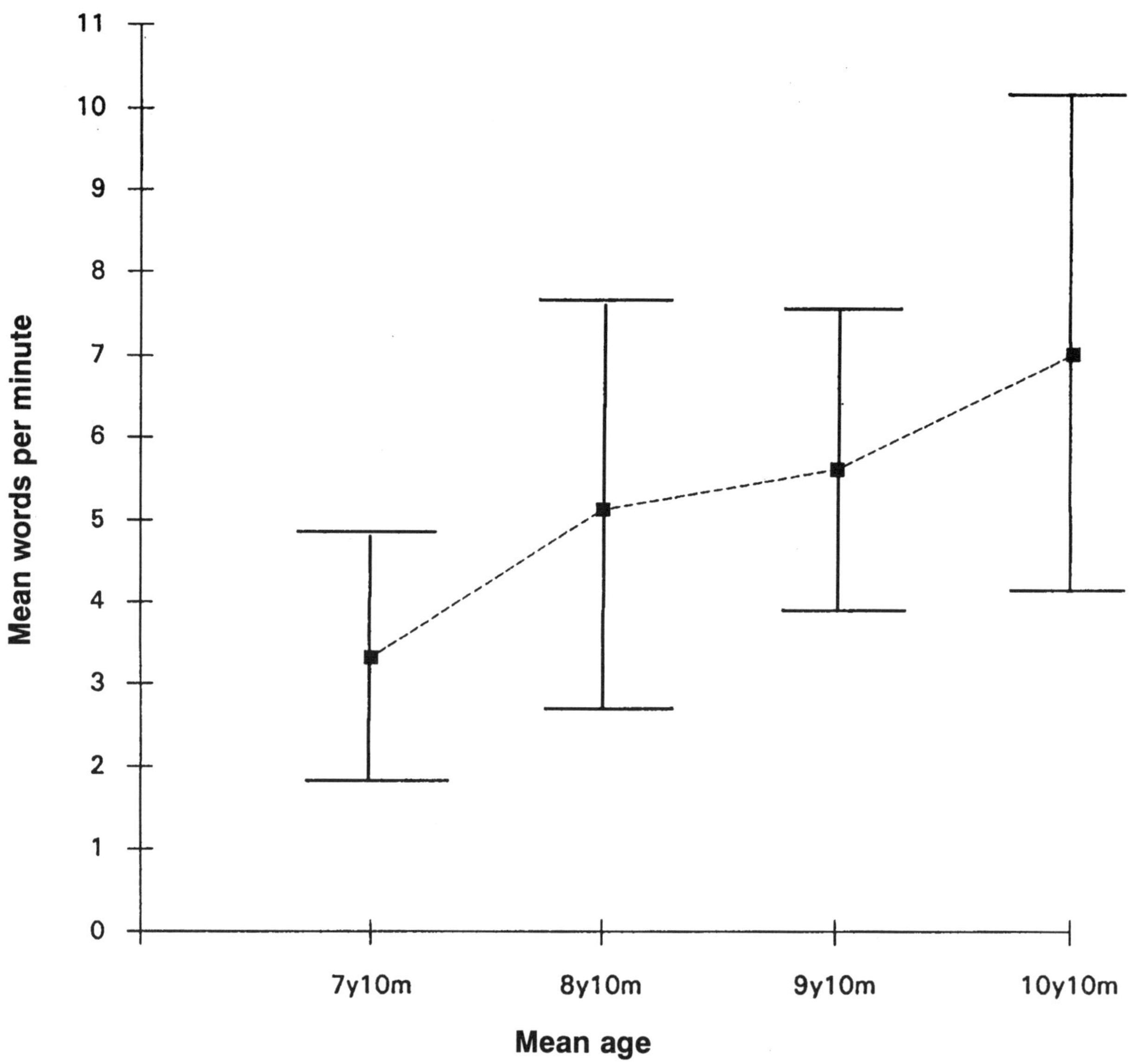

Figure 39 - Cheshire Primary Schools boys (N=82). Writing output over 20 minute period (mean; SD).

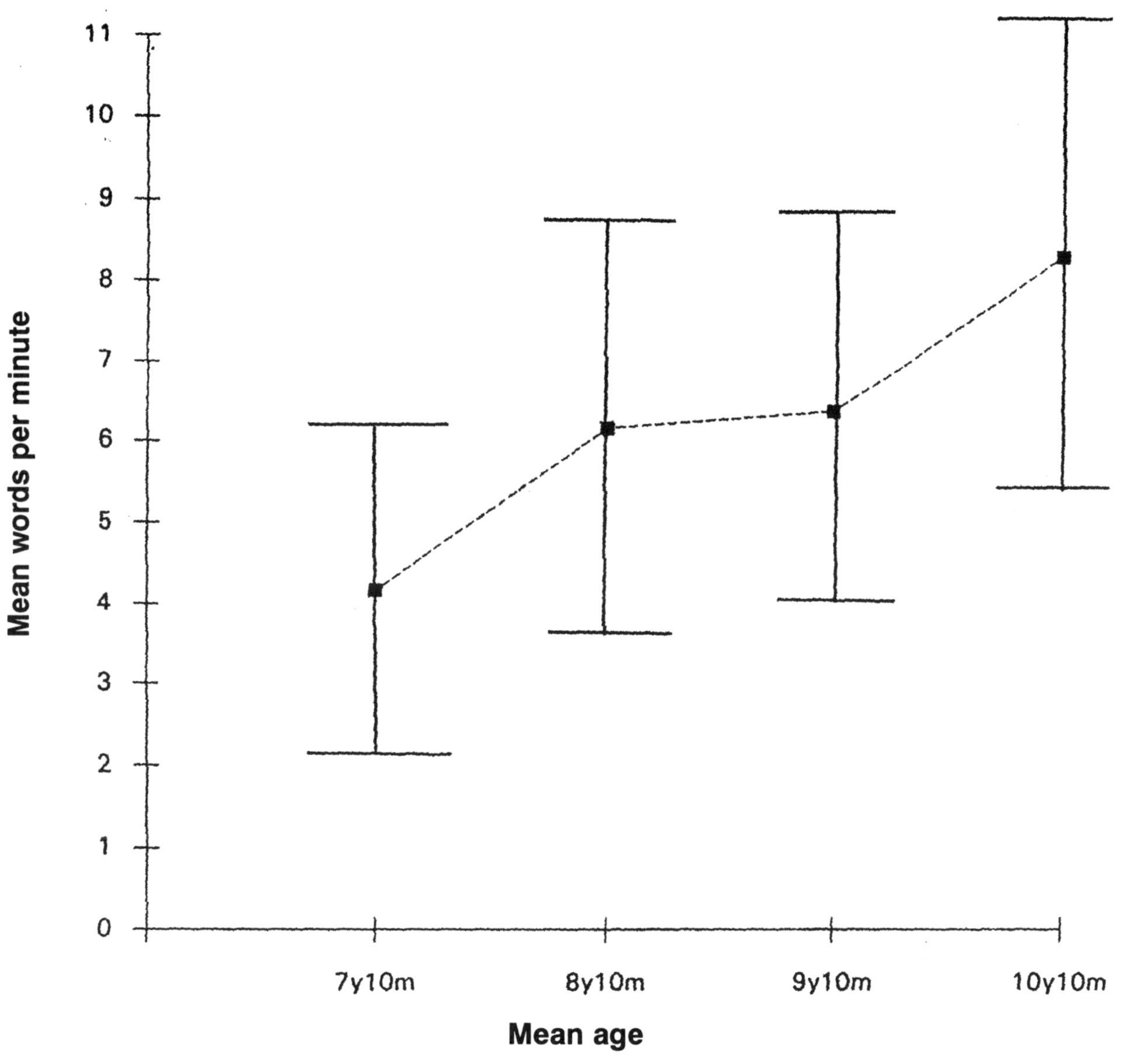

Figure 40 - Cheshire Primary Schools girls (N=86). Writing output over 20 minute period (mean; SD).

Words Per Minute: Summary

Mean Age:	**7:10**		**8:10**		**9:10**		**10:10**	
	Mean	**S.D.**	**Mean**	**S.D.**	**Mean**	**S.D.**	**Mean**	**S.D**
Girls	4.17	2.09	6.15	2.62	6.36	2.46	8.28	3.01
Boys	3.32	1.56	5.14	2.54	5.62	1.92	7.02	3.16
Total	3.76	1.91	5.63	2.61	5.98	2.22	7.64	3.14

Table 2 - Cheshire Primary School Pupils 19 schools; 168 pupils; 86 girls; 82 boys. Writing output: 20 minute period. This shows the means and standard deviations for each age group and for girls, boys, and total pupils, in terms of words per minute over the 20 minute period.

Case Study

The standardised writing task can provide a range of evidence not always apparent from general writing activities. *Figure 41* shows the writing of a right handed boy, aged 9 years 5 months, who writes about 'My Favourite Person'. The analysis which follows indicates the scope of information available from the standardised writing task. It is carried out for general writing output, handwriting and spelling. These are the skills most closely related in this task, as handwriting quality and spelling competence are the skills likely to influence the ability to put thoughts quickly on paper, particularly in the primary school years.

Writing output analysis

He writes 32 words in the 20 minute period (see asterisk in his writing), placing him in the lowest output levels for Year 4 pupils.

He writes 129 letters in the 20 minute period, which also places him in the lower output levels. Relatively speaking, his letter output is better than his word output, indicating that he writes relatively long words and is on the way towards becoming a more competent writer. He writes at the rate of 1.6 words per minute during the 20 minute period. His writing rate in considerably more than one standard deviation below the mean, indicating that his teacher should be monitoring his written output closely. His newly acquired joined script may be temporarily limiting written output; script and output should be monitored at regular intervals.

Handwriting analysis

There is evidence that all letters are correctly formed and that letter joins are developing well. Excessively long strokes are employed for letter joins, so that letters are widely spaced. Advice about how to leave the ends of letters quickly, forming sharp curves towards the beginning of the next letter (usually the top of the letter), will help to reduce joining space, and improve legibility (which comes from the tops of letters). With these changes, writing speed will also increase.

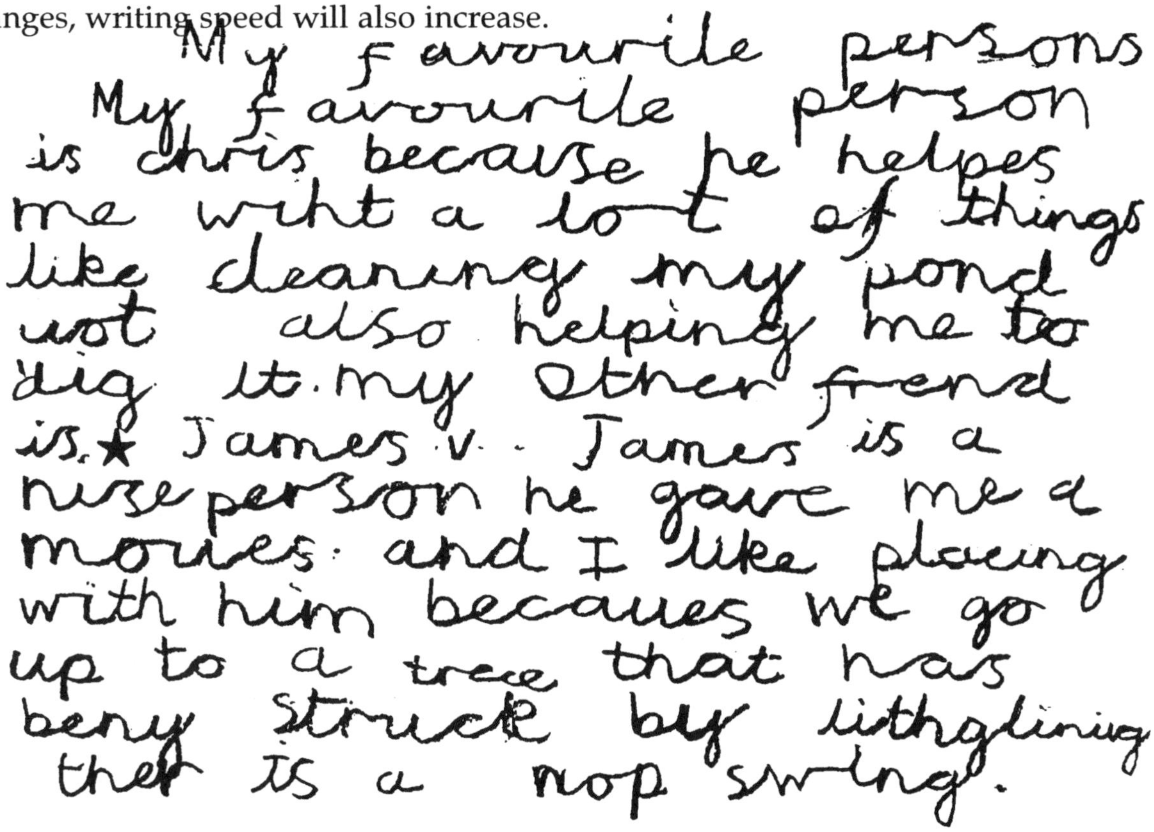

Figure 41 - A sample of writing by a right-handed boy, aged 9 years 5 months.

Spelling analysis

He writes a total of 67 words in all, spelling 39 different words correctly and 12 words incorrectly.

Incorrectly spelt words are:

helpes	
wiht	
uot	Key Word 'out'
frend	
nise	
moues	
plaeing	
becaues	Key Word 'because'
beny	Key Word 'been'
lithgtinig	
ther	Key Word 'there'

rop

Spelling recommendations

- He would benefit from a Key Word spelling programme.

- Because of insecurity in letter sequencing within words, he needs a strategy which encourages sound/symbol involvement, i.e. a multisensory programme for the learning of spelling. The following strategy would help him to succeed:

  - **write** the word correctly;
  - **say** the word clearly;
  - **write** the word **naming** each letter as he writes it;
  - **cover** the word;
  - **write** the word **naming** each letter as he writes it;
  - **check** the word;
  - **say** the word clearly.

The above sequence should be repeated until the word is known well.

CHAPTER 16

Computers as an Aid to Writing

In the *Code of Practice on the Identification and Assessment of Special Educational Needs* (DFE, 1994), it is suggested that at Stages 1 to 3 and before a Statutory Assessment has been initiated, for pupils with general learning difficulties:

> 'the LEA should consider the action taken by the school and should ask whether the school has explored the possible benefits of, and where practicable secured access for the child to, appropriate information technology, for example word processing facilities, overlay keyboards and software, providing training in the use of that technology for the child, his or her parents and staff, so that the child is able to use that technology across the curriculum in school, and wherever appropriate, at home'. (Para. 3:58)

For pupils with specific learning difficulties such as Dyslexia, the *Code of Practice* has a similar school and LEA requirement, though for these pupils there is special reference to the provision of word processing facilities, spell-checkers, and other software.

Since publication of the *Code of Practice* and its implementation in September 1994, pupils who would benefit from the introduction of information technological aids should have their needs explored and met before a Statutory Assessment is initiated and probably without need for a Statement of Special Educational Needs.

Although there is no specific reference to Dyspraxic pupils in the *Code of Practice,* there is likely to be at least one dyspraxic child in most classrooms.

The term ***dyspraxia*** means dysfunction of movement. It replaces the term ***clumsy,*** which was used to describe affected children throughout the 1980s. One cause of movement difficulties may be poor muscle tone, which affects pencil hold, posture, and most physical activities. All physical behaviour requires movement to some degree, though affected children may not have difficulty in all areas of movement. Some will experience speech/articulation difficulties in their early years, continuing longer than is usual. Virtually all have difficulty with handwriting, and most experience difficulty with drawing, physical education and games.

Many dyspraxic children are good readers, whose specific literacy difficulty is in handwriting. However, spelling achievement may be lower than expected because spelling can be influenced by poorly established letter formation and other handwriting characteristics.

The Dyspraxia Trust is an active body of parents and professionals who are concerned to make the children's plight known, and who are able to offer advice to teachers and parents. Virtually all such children have handwriting difficulties which will require comprehensive investigation and provision under the new *Code of Practice* requirements.

For pupils across the complete ability range, it is not possible to make any comprehensive statement about writing in the 1990s without reference to information technology for general classroom use. In schools, the range of computers with word processing facilities is very wide indeed, and lap top computers are becoming commonplace. In the early years of provision, many schools had BBC and/or Archimedes computers, though the range has now been widened considerably, particularly in large secondary schools. Computers with printing facilities give all pupils access to writing as a means of communication.

Word processing can be either an enabling system or can act as a supplement for the school's writing programme. Able writers will see word processing as a means of drafting, redrafting, editing, and ultimately as a means of producing a finished product worthy of display in school or other public place. Interest in managing the written word, and better control over what is written, are all increased by the adult appearance of the printed format. All lead to the encouragement of an editorial approach, giving the whole act of writing a professional flavour.

For less proficient writers, the word processor is a means of making their writing more acceptable, and worthy of being read by themselves and others. It is a way of developing pride in one's work and at the same time improving self-concept, for writing can be seen to be a bit of oneself that is permanently available for others to observe, to praise or to criticise.

Word processing can, with the exception of handwriting, encourage all of the skills embraced in this book. As well as word-processing software, there are programmes to improve spelling, punctuation, and grammatical skills. 'Spell checkers' are an integral facility of many word processing programmes.

The relationship between writing and information technology

1. Information technology can be a useful supplement to general writing skills for all children. It aids presentation and provides an easy facility for drafting, revising and editing.

2. The computer screen can be observed by two or three children at the same time, enabling 'conferencing', discussion about what they have written. Some programmes have enlarged type face or allow one to vary type face size. The larger type face is suitable for 'conferencing' or for pupils who need the larger type because they are poorer readers, are visually handicapped, or would benefit for other reasons.

3. Information technology provides a new beginning or extra stimulus for those who have had writing difficulties in the early stages. There is now considerable evidence that, so long as keyboard skills are also taught, the use of word processing facilities can unlock skills in formerly reluctant writers. The enthusiasm for writing has been shown not to be a passing fancy but has, for most pupils, carried them forward into new writing performance levels and attitudes.

4. Information technology can be particularly helpful for those with handwriting difficulties, i.e. have difficulty forming letters and letter joins, or have spacing and letter directionality problems.
   However, both handwriting and keyboard/word processing skills must be learnt. Word processing should, in most cases, aid conventional writing rather than supplanting it.

However, the fact that word processing errors can be easily corrected makes it an attractive medium for those with problems.

5. Facilities such as extended keyboards, overlay keyboards with touch sensitive pads, switches, joy stick, and mouse controls, make word processing easier than other forms of writing for many handicapped children. Pupils with physical, sensory and general intellectual impairment can usually benefit from the numerous adaptations available. For those with speech and language problems, the newer 'voice over' computer facilities are of unprecedented benefit.

6. Many word processing and desk top publishing packages allow one to add pictures to the text, to change the format and the fonts, and to generally construct a professional looking document or publication. Pupils see themselves as working within a medium which gives them much more potential than one in which writing alone is the only tool.

7. Some computers allow the colour of the text and/or the colour of the background to be varied. Some writers, especially those with visual impairment, find that different colour combinations suit them better than others, and are able to vary them accordingly.

8. For slow writers or for those with specific written language and spelling difficulties, schools may eventually wish to request special examination arrangements such as word processing facilities or extra time. The examination boards are concerned that the pupils' modes of working should be well established for class and coursework long before examination times approach and before special arrangements are requested. This is a further reason for exploring facilities for word processing early in the pupils' educational careers. The Scottish Examination Board already allows *any* candidate to use a word processor system provided it has no data storage device or spellchecker installed and it does not disrupt any other candidate. It is highly likely that this facility will be introduced by English examination boards in the relatively near future.

Different and sometimes contradictory advice has been given about the learning of conventional/typing keyboard skills for word processing. However, as the teaching of keyboard skills to pupils of all ages has become more commonplace, the evidence in favour of establishing them early is becoming available. Studies conducted principally in the USA have examined the outcomes when keyboard skills have been taught to children as young as six years of age. The general conclusion is that, without keyboarding skills, the vast potential of the computer/word processor is restricted. In controlled observation over a longer period of time, short and longer term effects of neglect of keyboard skills are as follows:

a. In the short term, the amount of keyboard writing is considerably restricted: descriptions are shorter and the overall written volume is less.

b. In the longer term, inefficient word processing habits are established and are resistant to change.

In fact, the problems that arise through lack of, or poor, keyboarding skills have a very similar impact to those of poor handwriting. When skills are reduced in either medium, children write less and never develop complete control over the written word. Beverly Scheib, who has reviewed current evidence on the teaching of keyboarding skills, suggests that when once knowledge of the 26 letters of the alphabet is established, unless there are exceptional circumstances, the teaching of keyboard skills can be only beneficial. Early instruction can be very simple, such as the placing of a coloured strip down the middle of the keyboard so that at least the appropriate hand is utilised for each keyboard half. The Fairley House Keyboard Training Programme, designed by Scheib, is one of the several keyboarding programmes now reaching the software market. It is available for use on BBC, Archimedes, and IBM compatible 3.5 and 5.25 inch range software, and can be obtained from:

Beverly Scheib, 1 D'Abernon Drive, Cobham, Surrey, KT11 3JE.

Many software producers have explicit catalogues and some will send software on approval to schools. The organisations SEMERC (Special Education Micro-electronic Research Centre) and ACE (Aids to Communication in Education) are available to help, and The Dyslexia Computer Resource Centre will advise on computers and software for pupils with specific learning difficulties. The National Council for Educational Technology (NCET) has government funding, conducts research, and will also give advice. CENMAC (Centre for Micro-assisted Communication) is particularly helpful with advice for handicapped children.

Useful addresses are:

Northwest SEMERC,
Fitton Hill CDC,
Rosary Road,
Oldham,
OL8 2QE
Tel: 0161 627 4469

The ACE Centre,
Ormerod School,
Waynflete Road,
Headington,
Oxford,
OX3 8DD
Tel: 01865 63508

The Dyslexia Computer Resource Centre,
Department of Psychology,
University of Hull,
Hull,
HU6 7RX
Tel: 01482 465589/465388/465157

Northern ACE Centre,
Park Dean School,
St. Martin's Road,
Fitton Hill,
Oldham,
OL8 2PY
Tel: 0161 627 1358

National Council for Educational Technology (NCET),
Milburn Hill Road,
Science Park,
Coventry,
CV4 7JJ
Tel: 01203 416994

Centre for Micro-assisted
Communication (CENMAC),
Charlton Park School,
London,
SE7 8HX
Tel: 0181 316 7589

CHAPTER 17

Assessing and Guiding Written Work: Resources for Teachers

Far too little attention has been paid, particularly in the 1960s, 1970s, and early 1980s to the formalities of writing. In some schools and local education authorities, neglect has spanned several decades, quite long enough to produce pupils, parents and teachers who know little about the craft of handwriting, discipline of accurate spelling, conventions of punctuation and grammar, and even the more individual aspects of expressive writing and style. The purpose of this section is to provide the reader with a number of publications whose contents can be used in two ways: firstly as a source of information about language structures, spelling, handwriting, and so forth, and to assist in examination of written work; secondly as a source for teaching, so that those elements can be discussed with pupils at appropriate stages of their writing development.

National Writing Project

The *National Writing Project*, initiated in 1985 and eventually taken under the wing of the National Curriculum Council in 1989, redressed the balance with regard to writing for expression and communication. The emphases of the wide range of authors tended to be on emergent writing, the writing environment, inventive spelling and more general attention to nurturing each child's natural and emerging abilities. Writing for learning was one of the more constructive *Writing Project* elements, and there are particularly useful articles in the dissemination books, 'Writing and Learning' and 'Ways of Looking'. Projects to develop home school writing partnership, and suggestions for creating links with the wider community, made valuable contributions in the late 1980s. The general policy of the *National Writing Project* was perhaps best summed up by Pam Czerniewska, National Writing Project Director, who stated: 'Writing project publications will enable teachers to discuss, reflect on and promote ways of fostering the competence and confidence of young writers'.

The National Writing Project journal, *About Writing*, was published between 1985 and 1989. Selected contributions were supplemented and new ones written for an extensive range of dissemination books, are published by Nelson.

The view taken by the current author, is that for children who do not have literate backgrounds, and for those who find reading, writing and spelling inordinately difficult, more early learning structure is required. Confidence can be engendered through two major aspects of classroom policy: encouraging writing, and valuing what pupils produce is an extremely important one; the other, crucial to less able writers, is to ensure that basic literacy skills are taught economically and correctly. 'Economically', means as early as possible, so that not too much time in the later years is spent on teaching and correcting handwriting, spelling, punctuation and grammatical skills. Children know whether their writing is of an acceptable standard, whether they really can write or spell, and whether praise is really warranted. They also tend to accommodate to whatever standards are expected, and this can be seen in the differing performance levels between top juniors from different primary schools when they go on to secondary education.

Rediscovering Grammar

Rediscover Grammar by David Crystal, was published in paperback at a reasonable price, by Longman in 1988. It could be described as the teacher's easy guide to understanding and putting right the idiosycracies of children's speech and writing. Presentation is excellent, with each of 76 concise sections devoted to an aspect of our language. It is often quite surprising to see a written explanation of many language structures which the majority of people seem to absorb with little actual instruction, and that adults often take for granted. Just a little correction here and there as the young child develops speech and language, seems to suffice.

To those who do not develop language 'naturally', we do a disservice if we do not help them to learn correct structures in their early school years. For example, young writers will transfer their confusion of 'much' and 'many' to written language, writing sentences such as 'there were much toys' or 'How much days till Saturday?' The section on 'count and noncount nouns' gives examples that can be employed to correct the problem. The concise information can then be utilised as the teacher chooses.

Excessive use of capital letters is a common feature of writing in primary pupils. It can result from a misunderstanding of what a sentence is, and the need for a capital letter at the beginning of the first word. Sometimes capital letters and sentences are so misunderstood that a capital letter is used for the beginning of each new line of writing. However, in older pupils, confusion is more likely to occur because of lack of knowledge about common and proper nouns, the former begins with a small letter and the latter with a capital, which can be clarified with the help of Section 29 of Crystal's text.

Are *you* really sure that 'old and oldest' are the regular forms of comparison, but that 'elder and eldest' are used when referring to family members? How often do newspaper reporters refer to the youngest, eldest or oldest son, when it is clear that there are only two sons, so that younger or elder are the correct forms?

The form of Crystal's text also makes it very suitable for older pupils needing a reference book for personal writing and/or for more formal examination purposes.

Grammar made easy

For a systematic programme on understanding and teaching grammatical skills, *Grammar Made Easy* by Barbara Dykes is an excellent source. This is a 1992 edition of an earlier publication, but it has a very up-to-date look in both presentation and ease of access. Published in Australia by Hale and Iremonger, it is available in the United Kingdom from Special Educational Needs Marketing, Newport, Shropshire. Sections on the main grammatical constructs really are easy to read and absorb, so that each part of speech (noun, pronoun, verb, adjective, adverb and preposition) is lucidly presented in as few pages as possible. Twelve prepositions, for example, are presented on two pages with a suitable illustration. More complex aspects of grammar are examined later in the book, for example, regular and irregular verbs and complements. The punctuation sections are concise and explicit.

Part Five, 'Get it right', has two sections: 'Some common mistakes explained' and 'Know the difference'. The latter explains the difference between words such as already/all ready, alright/all right, affect/effect, compliment/complement, and principle/principal.

The strength of the book is that a large amount of quite complex information is presented in a very simple manner. If we are able to clear up some of the confusion by ten or eleven years or so, particularly in the more able children, many errors which prove difficult to eradicate later may be avoided.

Each of the book's five parts has exercise examples to ensure that the reader understands what has been read. The same exercises can be used and supplemented by the teacher if they and further examples are required for pupils.

Dictionaries

Vocabulary development is an important aspect of pupils' writing. Children who limit their vocabularies to the words they believe they can spell correctly can be found in all classrooms.

Dictionaries have traditionally been either word books with pictures for younger children or those which are too complex for pupils with learning difficulties. However, learning the alphabet is now a requirement of the National Curriculum (Attainment Target 2, Level 1), and the use of an easy to use dictionary provides practice for alphabet skills. Schofield and Sims' dictionaries are relatively cheap and particularly well presented, often with different colours to emphasise the words, large print and good spacing. However, although these characteristics make for easy reference, they do not make the publications appear immature in other ways, i.e. they will not be objected to by the sophisticated or older pupil. The following publications can be recommended.

The *Concise Junior Dictionary* (published by Schofield and Sims) offers 5,000 words with simple definitions and 'a minimum of technical jargon'. Pronunciation is explained simply for any word which may cause difficulty, e.g. 'gaol' (say 'jail'), which also appears under 'jail', of course. The dictionary words are attractively highlighted in black on a light red background, and the definitions really are in words which are as simple as possible. Although the publishers direct the dictionary to 7 to 9-year-olds, the format and the content make it quite suitable for older less able writers.

Better Words: A First Thesaurus (published by Schofield and Sims) provides pupils with a choice of over 8,000 words, and aims to enrich vocabulary in both the spoken and written word. The superb format, with large initial capital and small letter at the head of each page, main word in red, and alternative words in black, make this publication an attractive one to use. Whilst the general appearance of this thesaurus makes it suitable for junior pupils of all ages, the care that has been taken with spacing and lay out makes it particularly suitable for less able writers. Even the recognition that there are alternatives to the word that first comes to mind may be a new concept for some writers. There are simple sections on *opposites* and *parts of speech.*

A Basic Dictionary (published by Schofield and Sims) is directed at 8 to 11-year-olds, and 11,000 words is rather a lot for less able writers. However, if they are introduced to the advantages of dictionary use from an early age, and given an attractive but easy one to begin with, some will progress to this publication. The main word appears in heavy black type and the definitions are short and simple. There is special help for pronunciation through use of capitals in stressed syllables.

A multi-sensory approach

The Hickey Multisensory Language Course (Second Edition) by Jean Augur and Suzanne Briggs, was published by Whurr Publishers in 1992. Although a paperback, the price is relatively high. However, this is a source book for teachers who may use it for one of two purposes. Its main purpose is as a guide for those who wish to be completely faithful to the Kathleen Hickey multisensory language course for the teaching of reading and writing. This faithful adherence is considered by many to be essential for dyslexics, i.e. for those with specific reading, writing and spelling problems. An alternative use for this publication is as a source for all teachers of written language. Its excellent index ensures that it can be used to great effect in this way. For example, the teacher who believes his or her pupil has a problem with 'ous' and 'us' is invited, through the index, to turn to page 433. Pages 433 and 435 give details of reading and spelling cards for teaching these elements, but also a story with questions, and extensive lists of words which have 'ous' or 'us' as syllables or suffixes.

Chapter Two should be read for the programme's rationale, as the title 'A pupil's need for simultaneously seeing, hearing, speaking and writing when learning the written language skills' suggests. The stimulus response routine, also described in this section, reflects good psychological learning theory, based on both Pavlovian and Skinnerian approaches. How little use we have made of those theories as teaching approaches have developed!

Chapter Four, 'The alphabet and dictionary', has ideas useful for pupils of all ages. Use of wooden or plastic letters is advocated for the exercises. However, Galt's sets of wooden small or capital letters are preferable to plastic ones, as the 'feel' of wooden letters gives pupils considerably more tactile experience than letters made from plastic.

So many of our poor writers show poor syllabification in their spelling errors, and have very poor understanding about the necessity of including vowels. They are often given insufficient guidance about when an encountered vowel can be expected to 'say' its short or long sound (simple sound or name). Chapter 6 will allow the teacher to reduce his or her own uncertainty about syllabification, and to recognise that syllable theory can be used beneficially with the general population of pupils who have reached the age of seven, or so, years. Using hand or pencil to 'beat out' the syllables in each word is an exercise in its own right and helps any child for whom word rhythm, length and sequence is an area of uncertainty.

Instruction on the teaching of each letter is accompanied by examples of the letter's place in lists of regular and irregular words, and by initial and final blends, prefixes and suffixes, as appropriate.

This book is an invaluable source for those wishing to understand the multisensory approach to the teaching of reading, writing and spelling. Much of the terminology, such as 'root' words, syllables, possession, regular and irregular words are known to teachers, and can be taught to pupils. However, the revised Hickey programme has many new ideas and concepts. It will be of value to any practising teacher who seeks to excel, and who is prepared to search for extra knowledge with which to assist those for whom learning to read and write is not an easy task.

Approaches to handwriting

Movement into Writing, written and published by Prue Wallis Myers, is a well-tried scheme that has been used for pupils aged 4 to 11 years. It is designed as a joined handwriting model from the beginning, rather than as joined writing which has been 'tacked on' to a print script model. Many recent schemes have been published to meet the early joining requirement of National Curriculum English. However, their authors have not understood that print script with letter exit strokes will not lead to a good joined/cursive hand. Unless the letter forms are correct from the beginning, pupils will write joined up print script which will quickly revert to print in the later junior and secondary school years. The Wallis Myers publications introduce letters conducive to writing flow from the beginning. Wallis Myers first letters are shown in the letter cards presented in Appendix B.

This scheme includes a set of large letters that can be used for developing correct letter movements and for word building at the early stages of reading and writing. The letters are on card, and are laminated to stand the wear and tear of being handled by children. Each set has 100 letters, with more of the commonly used letters, such as 'e', than of less commonly used ones. I see them as being quite useful for slow starters at top infant and early junior level. There is an *Animal Alphabet Story Book,* for use with younger children, which has each letter in line drawing, to encourage drawing and colouring practice. Each full page letter has a story to accompany it and to encourage recall of the letter for beginner writers.

The manual for this scheme, *Movement into Writing,* leaves nothing to chance, and there are sections that inform teachers about posture, hand movement, penhold, the requirements of left-handers etc. However, there is also a resource section which includes worksheets to encourage correct letter formation, and others to teach letter strings such as:

it at all ell ill in an ay ai

and consonant blends and digraphs such as:

bl br ch cr fl fr gl gr

The worksheets are accompanied by full instructions to the teacher, to ensure that movement patterns are correctly understood, rather than being simply copied from the worksheet image. Also available, is a simple, though well-constructed, sloping board, which can be very useful to avoid or correct poor pupil posture.

This scheme is available from the author, who has released it at cost price to ensure accessibility to schools in these times of financial economies. For further details contact:

P. Wallis Myers, 2 Richmond Court,
Richmond Road, Bowdon, Altrincham, WA14 2TZ
Tel: 061 928 1926

The Development of Handwriting Skills: A Resource Book for Teachers by Christopher Jarman was first published in 1979. Jarman's continuing experience and the observations of teachers have no doubt been incorporated in the revised edition, published by Simon and Schuster in 1993, and now marketed by Stanley Thornes of Cheltenham. Jarman is well-versed in the history of handwriting and in how the letters have evolved through the ages. Much of this knowledge is transmitted to the reader and influences the whole content of the book.

There is a section on handwriting development, with samples from different pupil age groups. Teachers are able to refer to them if they wish to make judgements about how their pupils are progressing.

Pre-writing patterns, discussion about lined or unlined paper, and a simple lined underlay, are helpful. A skeleton alphabet indicates slightly forward sloping letters so that, as in the Wallis Myers Model, the foundations for the development of a fluent written style are established from the beginning. There are then 51 photocopiable master sheets for letter patterns, letters, words, prose and poems that can be utilised to influence pupils' handwriting. The last 40 or so pages are devoted to ideas for project work, and suitable for use with more able pupils.

The Jarman *Handwriting Skills Photocopy Masters* are probably the most useful resource for work with less able writers. There are three books, in which worksheets are designed to move pupils through from useful mazes and patterns, which all incorporate a slightly sloping line and movement, and the essential component of anticlockwise oval movements, both of which are the basis for good letter formation. Exit strokes, ready for joins, are not introduced to the first letters, but are introduced gradually, first to 'l' and 't' and later to other letters such as 'd', 'n' and 'm'.

There are differences between the Wallis Myers and Jarman models, such as:

a. Myers shows how all letters can be joined, whereas Jarman advocates omitting joins from letters 'b', 'g', 'j', 'p', 's' and 'y', which end with a leftwards movement.

b. Jarman advocates a first '**k**' made up of straight lines, whereas Wallis Myers advocates the cursive '***k***' from the beginning.

Problems arise because neither of the authors has extensive experience of teaching pupils with special educational needs. There is a need for more resources and advice for those who are directly responsible for special needs pupils, and particularly for teachers whose pupils have already developed handwriting difficulties.

Handwriting Helpline by Jean Alston and Jane Taylor, was published by Dextral Books in 1990. The booklet suggests a cursive handwriting model to help those with handwriting difficulties, and deals with ten common problems. Usually the problems can be avoided if the correct teaching principles are adopted in the early stages of teaching. However, when problems have already developed, as the authors of this book have recognised, there is a need for teaching approaches to overcome them. The booklet is concise, and intended for easy reference by teachers or students. A ten point 'Rules round-up' provides an easy reference, so that principal difficulties can be identified and addressed without resource to unnecessary reading and practice.

The Handwriting Interest Group is a long established, non-profit making body of teachers, therapists, advisers and psychologists, who monitor and review current developments in handwriting. The group's aims are to:

- raise standards in the teaching of handwriting in schools;
- develop assessment techniques and teaching programmes for pupils with handwriting difficulties;
- disseminate teaching ideas and methods;
- encourage and coordinate research.

Members receive a journal and newsletter each year, and the opportunity to attend courses held in different locations throughout the UK. Contact is through the Hon. Secretary:

Felicitie Barnes, 6 Fyfield Road, Ongar, Essex, CM5 0AH.

Teaching spelling

There has been a recent revision of a publication by Charles Cripps and Margaret L. Peters, namely *A Hand for Spelling* (1991), published by LDA and *Catchwords: Ideas for Spelling,* (1990) published by Collins Educational, Harper Collins Publishers.

It reflects Margaret Peters' assertions in her earlier publication, *Diagnostic and Remedial Spelling Manual,* published by Macmillan in 1975, and revised in 1979, that spelling is a visual skill. LOOK-COVER-WRITE-CHECK is the strategy recommended for learning. To 'sound out' a word is to court disaster! A reference in the *Spelling Word Bank* (1978) states that 'there is no auditory strategy whatsoever'. The balance has been somewhat redressed by the motor element incorporated into *A Hand for Spelling.*

In a 1993 publication, *Spelling in Context,* Margaret Peters writes with co-author Brigid Smith. This is an attempt to examine Margaret Peters' views on the teaching of spelling in the context of an emergent literacy and inventive spelling philosophy. Look-Cover-Write-Check remains the predominant strategy, which I suggest is inadequate for writers who have inordinate spelling difficulties. Margaret Peters' diagnostic measures appear in a revised, though less objective, form. There are some useful ideas, such as the suggestion that very poor spellers might have a 'perfect writing book' in which they might practise known vocabulary every day, as a means of reinforcing knowledge of the words in their personal word banks. However, there is a limit to the number of days for which a strategy such as this could be employed. On the whole, this text does not provide sufficient teaching structure for weak or reluctant writers.

Teaching Spelling by Mike Torbe, published by Ward Lock in 1977, (revised 1995), offers a more balanced view of pupils' spelling strengths and weaknesses and of ways of dealing with them. While acknowledging his debt to the writings of Arvidson, Fernald, Peters and Schonell, he shows individuality of thought and is able to give a clear analysis of pupils' spelling errors, showing what individual weaknesses are likely to be. His assertion is that the two main reasons for pupils' inability to spell are that they experience either *weak visual memory,* or *weak auditory analysis*. He concedes, however, that weak visual memory is probably the most common cause. Torbe presents the teacher with strategies for the teaching of spelling, some basic teaching principles, recommendations for correcting and marking, and some teaching ideas and games.

Spelling Helpline by Jean Alston, published by Dextral Books in 1992 and revised in 1994, brings together Torbe's views on different spelling strengths and weaknesses, and those of Augur and Briggs, who revised the Hickey multisensory teaching programme. This is a concise booklet, written for easy reference for parents, teachers, and older students. Strategies for learning to spell are outlined for three types of writers: those with weak visual memory; those with weak auditory memory; and those who have little idea of the relationship between sound/sight/and symbol, in other words those who seem to be weak in both major channels. Methods of learning to spell are simply presented. The learning of 'Key Words' for spelling is advocated, with 'Key Words' available in checklists for easy pupil access and recording. A syllabic approach to teaching spelling is made available for those who may not have encountered that very useful and successful approach. The intention in writing this booklet was to make a few key principles available to those who need help with spelling. Above all, it draws attention to the fact that LOOK-COVER-WRITE-CHECK is too simple a learning strategy for those with inordinate difficulties. The author hopes to protect the student with severe spelling difficulties from the disappointment that sole reliance on the visual method could engender.

Easy Type By Ros Kinloch is a structured, multi-sensory, small step programme, that combines spelling development with the teaching of keyboard skills. It teaches through structured exercises, with spelling/typing sequences that are based on family word groupings, phonic blends and high frequency phrases and sentences. The material comes in four modules, which take pupils through hand-key exercises so that they become familiar with different parts of the keyboard and with frequently used keyboard sequences.

The teaching programme can be used with any keyboard or word processor, and does not require the teacher to have other specialist knowledge. It aims to build:

- keyboard familiarisation.
- typing/word processing skills.
- spelling awareness.
- fine motor movement and control.

It is A4 size with flip-over, wire bound top. It is suitable for pupils from Year 3 to Basic Adult Education, and is available from: Egon Publishers Ltd., Royston Road, Baldock, Herts, SG7 6NW.

Rescuing Spelling by Melvyn Ramsden, published by Southgate in 1993, takes an approach that can be complementary to all others and can add considerable interest and awareness of word meaning and structure for developing spellers. After informing about the philosophies of, and the strategies advocated by, other writers on the teaching of spelling, he writes at length about word origins and meanings. He bases his pupil spelling programmes on the following precepts:

- The English spelling system is logical and almost entirely self-consistent.
- 'Exceptions', far from being widespread, are extremely rare.
- There is a reason for every English spelling.
- English spelling is primarily the representation of **meaning**.

The text has many examples of how morphological relationships can be utilised in teaching. Pupils are to be introduced to 'matrices' and 'word webs' which show how words can be constructed and their parts separated for understanding of spelling logic. Central to word construction is the formula 'prefix - base word - suffix', though multiples of prefixes and suffixes can also be handled within this simple pattern. There are comprehensive lists of prefixes, suffixes, and of other aspects of written language that teachers will find useful for developing spelling skills, particularly in pupils who are beginning to make progress.

Getting it Write, written and published by Melvyn Ramsden in 1993, is intended as a companion text to *Rescuing Spelling*. Here we have many examples of how Ramsden's philosophy can be implemented with pupils and how 'matrices' and 'word webs' can be employed to develop pupils' understanding of the English spelling system. As well as the many examples of how pupils might be taught to use different letter sequences such as 'ch/tch' and 'ge/dge', there is a word index which allows the teacher to explore word or word part meanings further or to find a group of other words which illustrate the same structure for teaching purposes. Items in the second text, *Getting it Write,* are cross referenced with the earlier text *Rescuing Spelling,* so that the teacher has complete access to all the information that Ramsden is able to offer. All available information about word origins and meanings is, of course, available in any comprehensive dictionary. Ramsden's texts will encourage greater use of the dictionary which I suspect is greatly under-utilised in most areas of the educational curriculum.

Ramsden, like many other writers, tends to support only his own spelling philosophy and strategies. There is no doubt that interested teachers will learn a great deal from this author. However, I am inclined to believe that some of the established teaching media such as 'Key Words' and basic syllable structure also have their place. If all spelling philosophies and strategies are known to teachers, it is likely that each will have its use for different pupils at different stages of their spelling development and progress.

CHAPTER 18

Conclusion

The purpose of this book is to raise awareness of pupils' writing as a source of information about their progress, and to draw attention to ways in which standards can be raised through the development of different aspects of writing. During the 1980s there was a growing interest in children's writing from a composing, creative and expressive point of view. Ways of teaching the formal aspects of writing remained, principally based in writing exercises for practising word development, punctuation and grammatical skills. In this book, in order to redress the balance and bring punctuation, grammar and other formalities also into the realm of individual development, the emphasis has been placed on individual pupils' written output. With this approach, the formalities of writing can be examined and developed in a manner which is meaningful to the writer and relevant to the stage of progress already attained.

Ways in which pupils' written work can be examined, in both informal and formal manners have been suggested. It is not intended that the assessments and teaching programmes should be exhaustive. Only ideas which are manageable by busy teachers are described and only selective teaching objectives are presented. It is acknowledged that programmes such as these can only be put into practice for a number of pupils at any one time. However, if only one or two teaching objectives are followed each year, some pupils who would not otherwise have made progress, will do so. Although it has not always been possible to follow each writing sample with a precise teaching programme, the links between assessment and teaching have been established.

The resources referred to in Chapter 17 have been carefully selected. Some, such as the most recent publication by Margaret Peters inevitably has a place because, in the publications of the late 1960s and early 1970s, her work was seminal, and there have been many developments in the teaching of spelling which have emanated from it. Other publications, such as *Rediscover Grammar,* by David Crystal, are there because their authors are experts in their field and present information and ideas in a concise manner suitable for the busy teacher.

This book has been brought to life by the involvement of children and their willingness to commit words to paper, so that readers could use their writing as a focus for discussing different aspects of general writing skills. For this purpose, it was of great help to have the involvement of one primary school's pupils and staff during the 1992 and 1994 projects.

No one can pretend that the last word on the subject of pupils' writing has been written in these pages or elsewhere. The observations included here are intended as a stepping stone to improving the standards of written work, particularly for pupils in the middle and lower ranges of writing performance.

References and Further Reading

Alston, J. and Taylor, J. (1990) *Handwriting Helpline.* D. Paul, Dextral Books: Manchester.

Alston, J. (1990) *Aspects of handwriting in primary school children.* Unpublished Ph.D. thesis, University of Manchester.

Alston, J. (1994 Edn.) *Spelling Helpline.* D. Paul, Dextral Books: Manchester.

Alston, J. (1992) 'Assessing Writing Speeds', *Handwriting Review.* Available from F. Barnes, Handwriting Interest Group, 6 Fyfield Road, Ongar, Essex, CM5 0AH.

Arvidson, G. L. (1977) *Learning to Spell.* Pergamon: Oxford.

Arvidson, G. L. (1977) *Alphabetical Spelling Lists:* Nelson: Walton-on-Thames.

Assessment of Performance Unit (1991) *Assessment Matters: No. 4.* Evaluation and Monitoring Unit (EMU) of the School Examinations and Assessment Council.

Augur, J. and Briggs, S. (1992) *The Hickey Multisensory Language Course* (second edition). Whurr Publishers: London.

Burroughs, G. E. R. (1957) *Study of the Vocabulary of Young Children.* Educational Monogaph No. 1. University of Birmingham Institute of Education: Oliver and Boyd.

Cato, V., Fernandez, C., Gorman, T., Kispal, A., White, J. (1992) *The Teaching of Initial Literacy: How do teachers do it?* NFER: Slough.

Cripps, C. (1988, 1991) *A Hand for Spelling.* LDA: Wisbech.

Cripps, C. and Peters, M. L. (1990) *Catchwords: Ideas for Teaching Spelling.* Collins Educational; Harper Collins Publishers: Glasgow.

Croft, C. (1983) *Spell-Write: An Aid to Writing, Spelling and Word Study.* Wellington: New Zealand Council for Educational Research, P.O. Box 3237, Wellington 6000, New Zealand.

Croft, C. (1983) *Teachers Manual for Spell Write.* Studies in Education No. 34. New Zealand Council for Educational Research: Wellington.

Croft, C. (1992) *Guidelines, Combining Spelling with Writing in Primary Classrooms.* New Zealand Council for Educational Research: Wellington.

Crystal, D. (1988) *Rediscover Grammar.* Longman: Harlow.

Czerniewska, P. (Director) (1989-90) *National Writing Project Publications.* Nelson: Walton-on-Thames.

Department of Education and Science (1991) *Assessment, Recording and Reporting: A Report by H M Inspectorate on the First Year, 1989-90.* HMSO.

Department for Education (1994) *Code of Practice on the identification and assessment of special educational needs.* Central Office of Information: London.

Dolch, E. W. (1945) 'Basic Sight Vocabulary of 200 Words', *A Manual of Remedial Reading.* Garrard Press: Champaign, Illinois.

Dykes, B. (1992) *Grammar made easy*. Hale and Iremonger: Sydney: Available from Special Educational Needs (Marketing) Newport, Shropshire.

Dyspraxia Trust (1993) *Praxis Makes Perfect.* Available from: The Dyspraxia Trust, P.O. Box 1270, Gerrards Cross, Bucks, SL9 0SF.

Galt Toys Ltd. Capital Letter Templates; Lower Case Letter Templates. Cheadle, Cheshire.

Gates, A. I. (1937) *A Reading Vocabulary for the Primary Grades.* Teachers' College, Columbia University.

Hackett, G. (1989) 'Let's write a story', *Support for Learning,* Volume 4, No. 3, pp 153 - 159.

Hobson, E. W. (1980) *A Basic Dictionary*. Schofield and Sims: Huddersfield.

Jarman, C. (1995 Edn.) *The Development of Handwriting Skills,* Stanley Thornes: Cheltenham.

Macleod, I., McLaughlin, P., Anderson, A. (1989) *A Concise Junior Dictionary*. Schofield and Sims: Huddersfield.

Myers, P. Wallis. (1994) *Movement into Writing.* Available from: P. Wallis Myers, 2 Richmond Court, Richmond Road, Bowdon, Altrincham, WA14 2TZ.

National Writing Project, (1985-1989) *About Writing.* National Writing Project Newsletters. School Curriculum Development Committee: London.

New Zealand Council for Educational Research (1977) *Alphabetical Spelling Lists.* Nelson: Walton-on-Thames.

Peters, M. L. and Cripps, C. C. (1978) *The Word Bank Project: Teachers' Manual.* Macmillan: London.

Peters, M. L. (1979) *Diagnostic and remedial spelling manual.* Macmillan: London.

Peters, M. L., Smith, B. (1993) *Spelling in Context: Strategies for Teachers and Learners.* NFER-Nelson: Windsor.

Ramsden, M. (1993a) *Rescuing Spelling.* Southgate: Crediton, Devon.

Ramsden, M. (1993b) *Getting it Write.* Available from: 5 Le Bourg, Eynesse, 332200 Ste-Foy-La-Grande, France.

Scheib, B. (1993) *The design and implementation of a programme to teach keyboarding skills to children with specific learning difficulties.* Unpublished dissertation, University College of North Wales, Bangor.

School Curriculum and Assessment Authority. (1994) *English in the National Curriculum: Draft Proposals,* May. HMSO: London.

Torbe, M. (1995) *Teaching Spelling.* Ward Lock: East Grinstead.

Vernon, P. E. (1948) *A Preliminary Investigation of the Vocabulary of Scottish Children Entering School.* Scottish Council for Research in Education. Studies in Reading: Volume 1. University of London Press: London.

Vernon, P. E. (1977) *Graded Word Spelling Test.* Hodder and Stoughton: Sevenoaks.

Watts, A. F. (1944) *The Language and Mental Development of Children.* Harrap: London.

Windridge, C. (1985) *Better Words: A First Thesaurus.* Schofield and Sims: Huddersfield.

Assessing and Promoting Writing Skills

APPENDIX A

A Year 5, right handed, 10-year-old boy, writes a letter to the newspaper.

On the positive side:

- this boy is prepared to write at length, despite considerable difficulty in spelling and general writing skills;
- handwriting is, on the whole, legible;
- he writes in sentences using capital letters and full stops;
- from this sample, the boy's written word bank is as follows:

  I that the be by or to in and will then not so are as
  it is for there some thing done they put

  village police round streets stop cars houses much safer
  bad very safe now wood lane soon ever gets buy

- although words are often incorrectly spelt, each word has the correct number of syllables/sound beats.

Problems occur in:

- apart from 'village', 'police', 'safer' and 'houses', all correctly spelt words are of one syllable only;
- word spacing is variable;
- letter sizes are variable.

Teaching objectives in order of priority:

1. He needs a sound/symbol (multisensory) spelling programme, based on his spelling needs and beginning with common word groups such as:

should	driving	who
would	walking	what
	breaking	when
		why

When learning to spell he should:

a) **write** the word correctly;

b) **say** the word clearly;

c) **write** the word, naming each letter as he writes it;

d) **cover** the word;

e) **write** the word naming each letter as he writes it;

f) **check** the word;

g) **say** the word clearly.

If a small piece of paper is used for each word, it can be folded over each time the word is written.

2. Extra pencil lines should be drawn in his writing book to show a suitable height for 'x' height letters. This can be done on the occasional page to remind him to correct relative letter sizes.

3. When relative letter sizes are corrected, word spacing may spontaneously improve. If spacing does not improve, a cardboard finger, the same size as his more regular spacing should be provided.

4. Spelling progress should be monitored:

   - Key Word spelling should be checked

   - a syllable spelling programme should follow.

Assessing and Promoting Writing Skills

APPENDIX B

Master Sheets for Producing Alphabet Letter Cards
Alphabet Letter Cards devised by Jean Alston

Instructions for using Alphabet Letter Cards

The Large cards should be cut into letter cards: 10 letter or digraph cards per sheet, giving 30 small cards in total.

A reliable knowledge of letters of the alphabet is essential for all children. Until letter sounds and correct letter movements are known, children do not have the tools for reading and writing. The alphabet letter cards provide a way of teaching the letters and simple digraphs quickly and easily. Because the cards are easy to handle, and suitable for young children's hands, pupils themselves feel in control of the letters and ultimately of their own learning. Letters should be taught at the same time as early reading. Pupils can then make their own links as they develop an early reading and writing vocabulary.

Although letter cards can be used as the teacher wishes, there are ways of using them in which learning will occur more quickly. The child should see the complete set of cards in the teacher's or parent's hand. He or she should know that there are only 30 letters, or letter combinations, to learn The letters can be spread out, so that the number 30 does not seem too daunting. Letters are then taught one by one. (Note that x is not included because there is no suitable object with which to illustrate the letter.)

Letters can be introduced in any order. However, a simple and commonly used letter. such as c should be introduced first. The way in which each letter is taught is important. The sequence is as follows:

1. Show the child the side of the card which has a letter only.

2. Ask if he or she knows the sound the letter usually makes.

3. Say the sound of the letter.

4. Turn the card quickly (a half second after showing the side with the letter only).

5. Say the sound of the letter and the name of the object, e.g. 'cat'. Do NOT say 'c for cat'. The intrusion of 'for' makes the sound - picture association less effective.

6. The child can learn each letter sound as he is ready. Some children will learn only one letter each week. Others will learn three or more.

7. The cards should be shown to each child every day until learning is complete. All cards, even the learned ones, are included in the pack. The child gains confidence from knowing some cards before the new ones for learning are introduced. In this way, over learning also takes place.

The letter-only side of each card shows a small dot, indicating the correct starting point for each letter. Correct letter formation can be taught by encouraging the child to trace over each letter from its starting 'dot', first with index finger, then with pencil and also with different coloured crayons. Learning is more efficient if the child says the sound of the letter as it is written. In this way, maximum practice of each letter movement occurs, and speech and writing are coordinated.

For extra letter formation practice, the card showing the selected letter should be placed at the left margin of the writing book or paper. A line of practice in the formation of that letter is then encouraged.

Research has shown that, within reason, variable letter forms are acceptable to young children. Letters with or without joining flicks are easily identified. The alphabet letter cards have cursive letters, ready for joining, and are compatible with the requirements for early literacy suggested in National Curriculum English.

Letter names are required for learning to spell. When letter sounds and letter movements are learned, the child should be taught that everything and everybody has a name, and that each letter also has a name. Letter names can be used for the formal teaching of spelling.

The mastersheets included in this book will enable teachers to make their own sets of cards. However, sets of letter cards and instructions can be also obtained from: Dr. Jean Alston, 7 Harrington Drive, Gawsworth, Macclesfield, SK11 9RD, at £2.00 per set. £2.40 incl. postage and package. These letter forms also occur in *Movement in Writing,* a handwriting scheme available from: P. Wallis Myers, 2 Richmond Court, Richmond Road, Bowdon, Cheshire, WA14 2TZ (Tel: 0161 928 1926).

Assessing and Promoting Writing Skills

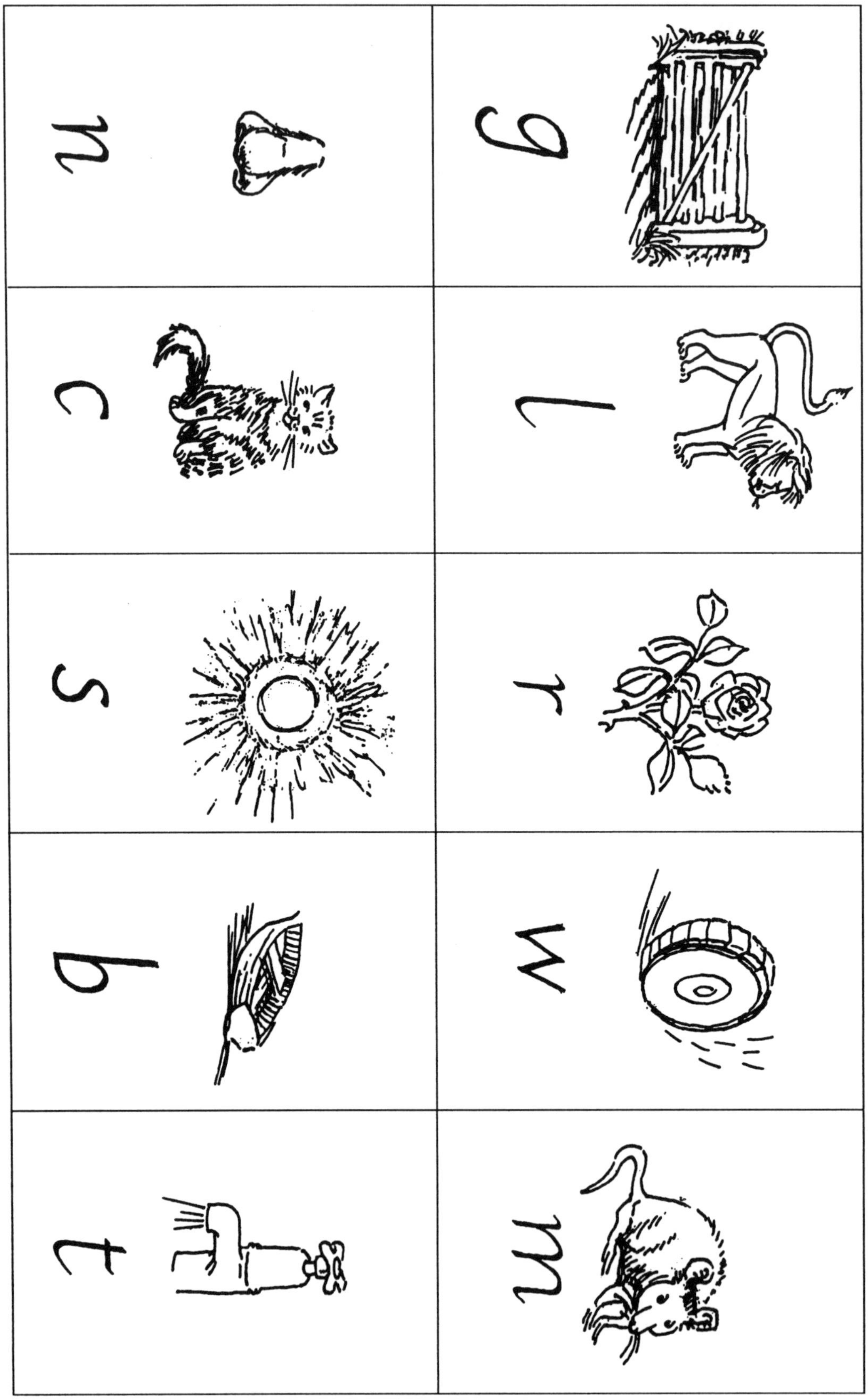

Assessing and Promoting Writing Skills

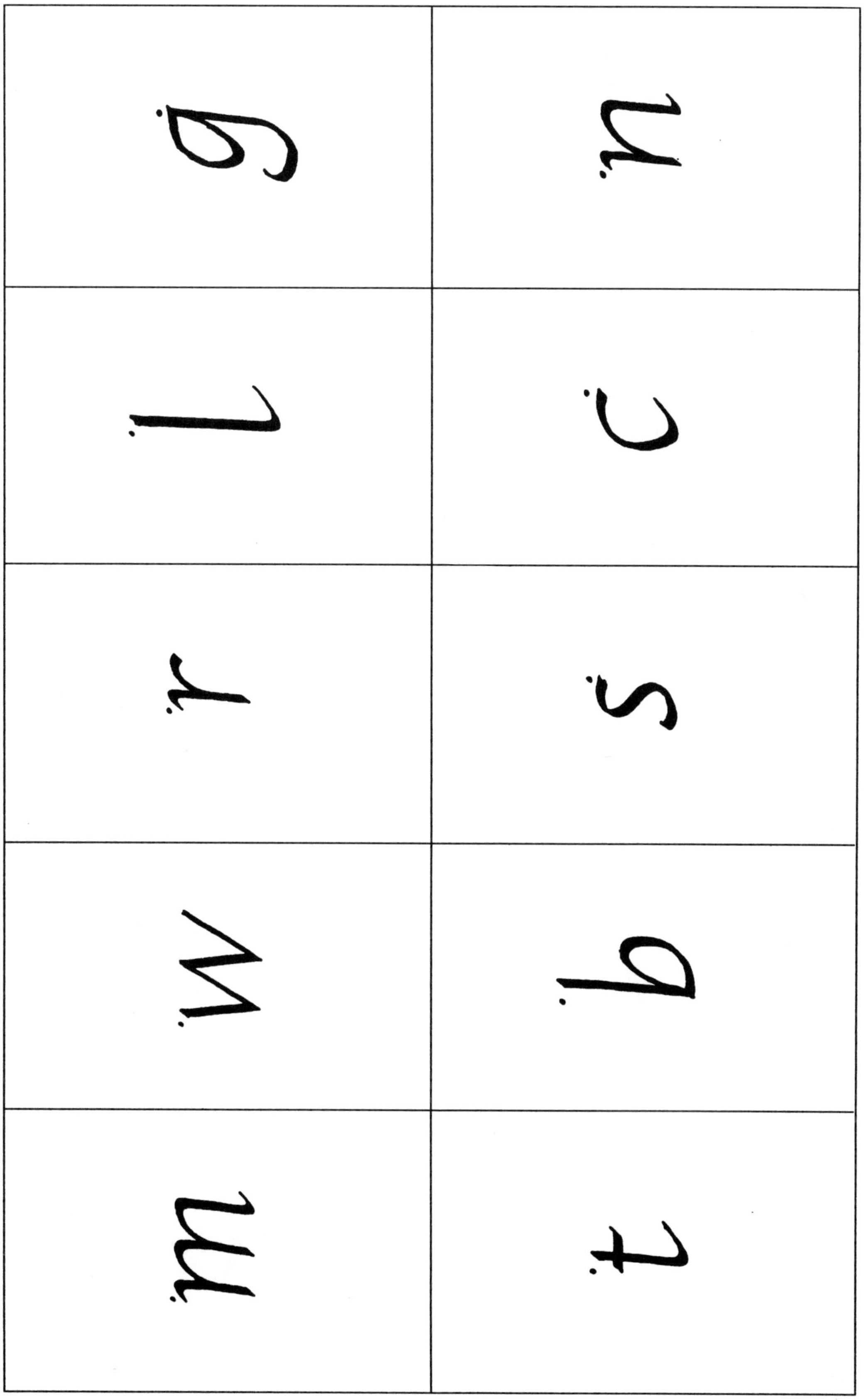

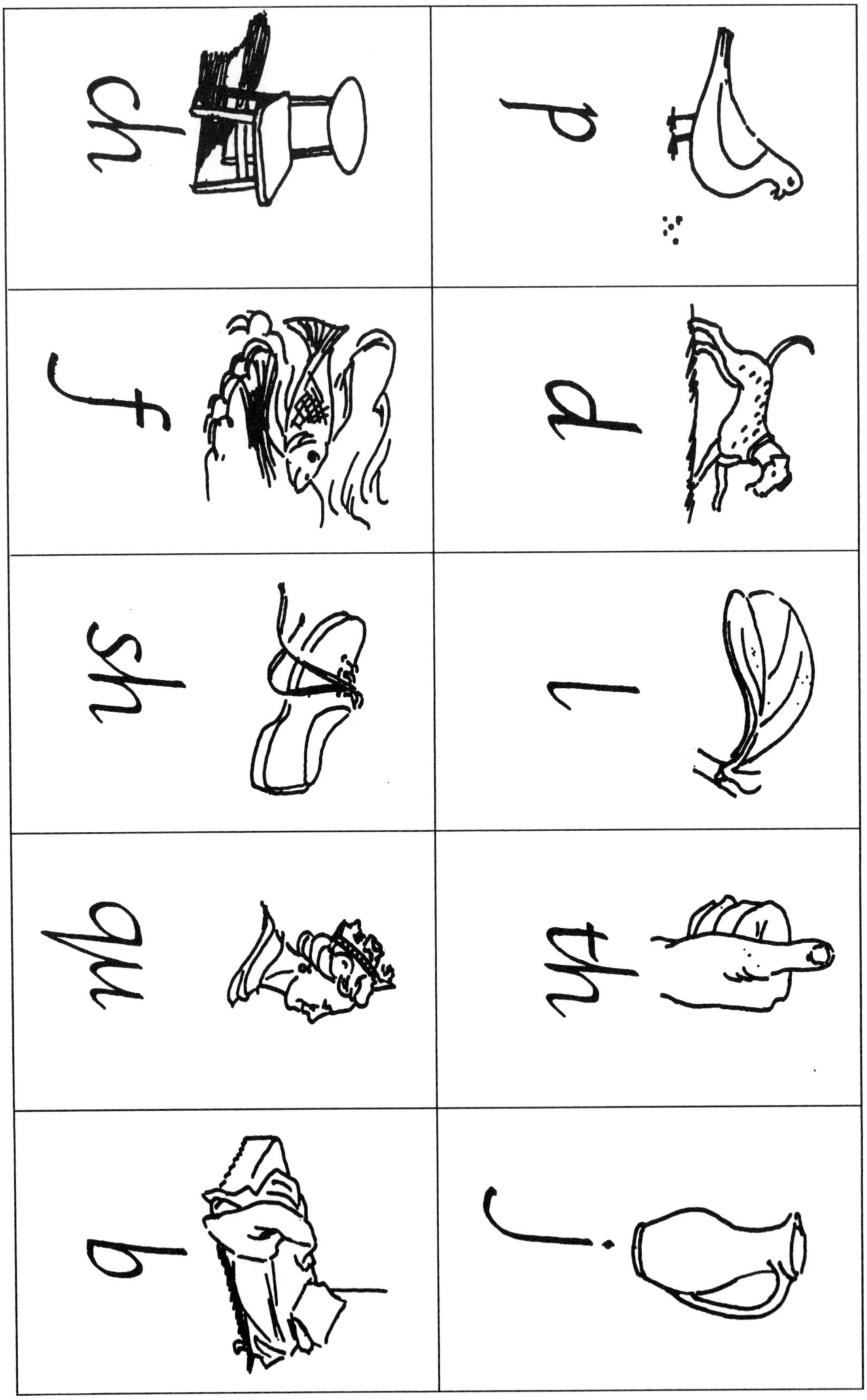
ch
p
f
d
sh
l
qu
th
b
j

p	ch
d	f
l	sh
th	wh
j	b

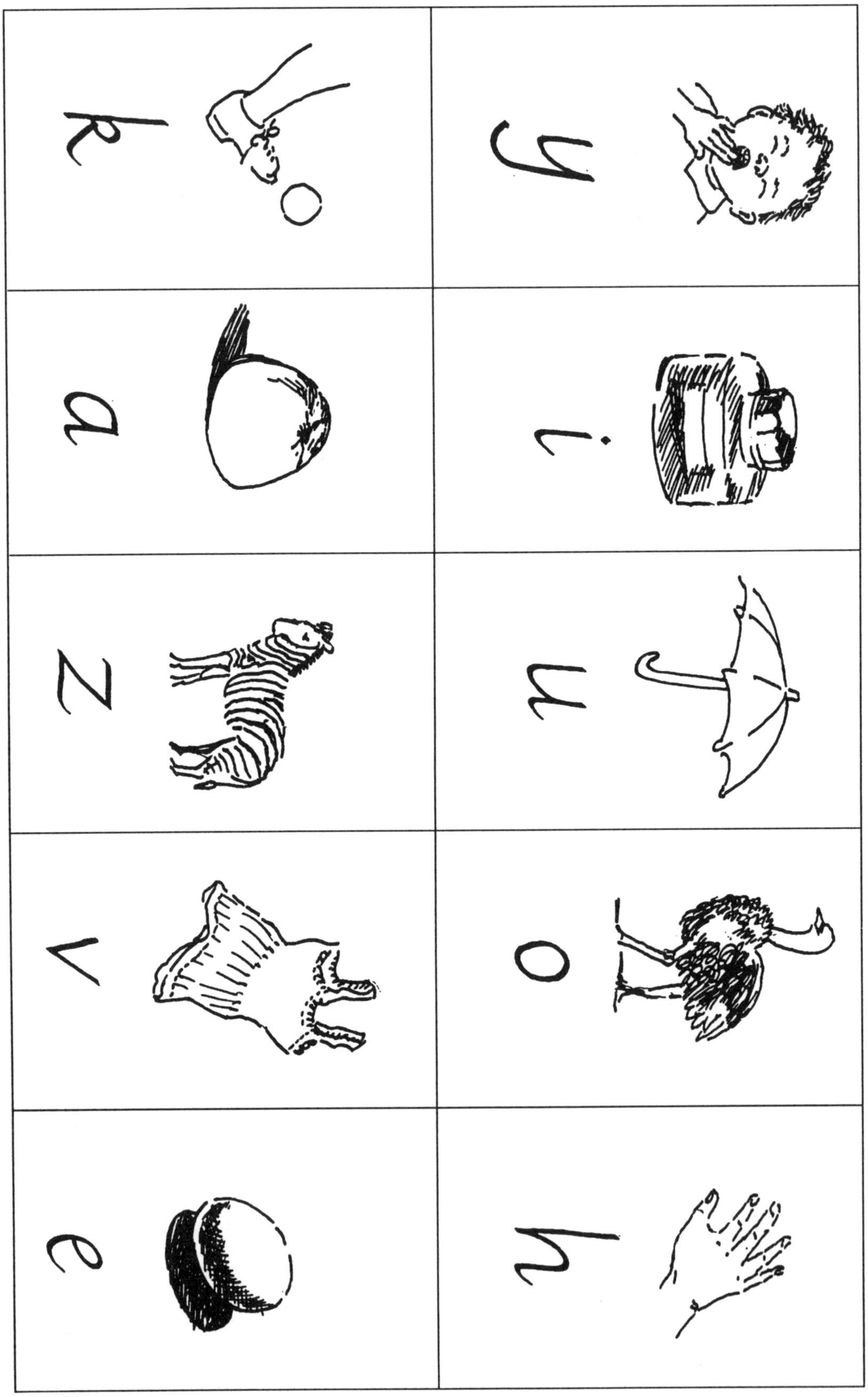
k
y
a
i
z
u
v
o
e
h

Assessing and Promoting Writing Skills

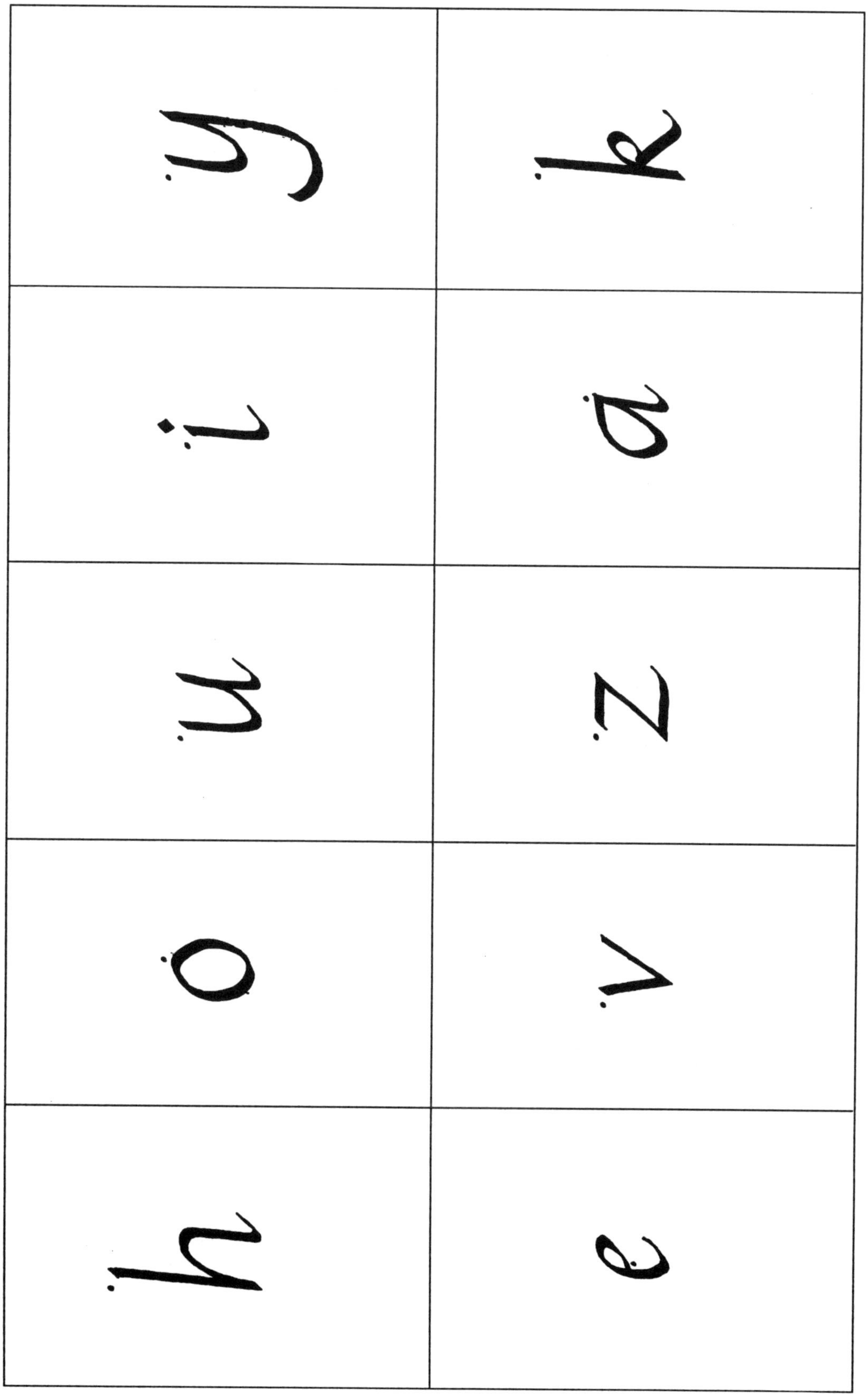

Assessing and Promoting Writing Skills

APPENDIX C

Master Sheets for Producing Lined Writing Paper Formats

It is suggested that these should be photocopied on to A4 paper. Two sheets with vertical lines ('portrait') and two sheets with horizontal lines ('landscape') are included to show that either plane is an option when children are writing.

Assessing and Promoting Writing Skills

Assessing and Promoting Writing Skills